D0907430

VISIONS OF JESUS

VISIONS OF JESUS

CHET & LUCILE HUYSSEN

LOGOS INTERNATIONAL
Plainfield, New Jersey

*All quotations from the Bible are taken
from the King James Version.*

VISIONS OF JESUS
Copyright © 1977 by Logos International
All rights reserved
Printed in the United States of America
Library of Congress Catalogue Card Number: 77-84183
International Standard Book Number: 0-88270-223-8
Published by Logos International, Plainfield, New Jersey 07061

Dedicated to
The Lord Jesus Christ
who so graciously gave these
visions to each one as recorded

And it shall come to pass afterward that I will pour out My Spirit upon all flesh; and your sons and your daughters shall prophesy, your old men shall dream dreams, your young men shall see visions; and also upon the servants and upon the handmaids in those days will I pour out My Spirit.

Joel 2:28-29
(King James Version)

CONTENTS

Acknowledgments

We wish to express our appreciation for the generous cooperation of all contributing authors, publishers, and the many friends who have graciously shared their experiences and visions with the readers of this book. We also thank our good friends, Doris Nylander who devoted much time to details and the typing of the manuscript, the Reverend Kent Nylander and Elizabeth Benson who have given wise counsel and encouragement.

If, in any instance, acknowledgment of any materials has been inadvertently omitted, the authors hope that they may be informed of the oversight so that proper credit may be given in future editions.

We pray that you will be blessed in your reading of this book.

Chet and Lucile Huyssen

Foreword

It is the hope of the authors, those who assisted in preparing the manuscript, those who read the testimonies, and those who contributed their experiences that these accounts of visions of Jesus will inspire many to believe in the living Jesus Christ as their personal Lord and Saviour and to know that He indeed is the same yesterday, today, and forever.

A vision is one of God's holy gifts and ministries to man. Over and over again we are assured in the Old and New Testaments that visions are views of realities, the unseen things which are eternal (2 Corinthians 4:18).

We feel that anyone who reads these accounts with an open heart may receive a blessing and will be thrilled to know that people from all walks of life have seen their Lord in vision. We praise God for the many changed lives that resulted from these visions and we give Him thanks that He continues to minister through these testimonies.

Introduction

This book is a collection of testimonies and accounts of those down through history who were blessed with a vision of Jesus. Some people have longed for years to see their Lord in a vision, others have had a revelation of Him without asking for it, and still others have seen our Lord without fully realizing the significance or purpose of the vision until years later.

While teaching junior high school students, I began collecting antique buttons, not only because I enjoyed doing so, but because I felt it would encourage my students to pursue hobbies. During this time I heard of a Methodist minister's wife, Genevieve Parkhurst, who had had a beautiful vision of Jesus and at the same time was miraculously healed of cancer. Soon afterward, I gathered accounts by Sundar Singh, Warner Sallman and Catherine Marshall of their visions of Jesus.

My heart was filled with awe and inexpressible joy as I read these accounts. Several questions crossed my mind. Was Christ appearing to many people? Were there others who had seen Him, and who were they? Thinking how beautiful it would be to collect testimonies of those who had seen Jesus in a vision, I soon gave up collecting antique buttons.

Being more and more impressed with the significance of these visions, I prayed, "O Lord, if You will show me more accounts of visions of Jesus, I will collect them for others to read so that they, too, might experience this tremendous joy that I have received." God answered that prayer: He graciously supplied books, magazines, testimonies and sermons that told of more visions. Those who had been blessed with visions included artists, housewives, ministers, agnostics, soldiers—people from all walks of life. Each new vision collected became like a jewel to be added to a beautiful necklace. Eventually, what I had gathered over a ten-year period for friends and family developed into manuscript form.

It was during this period that Dr. Frank C. Laubach encouraged my husband and me to organize literacy centers throughout the greater metropolitan Chicago area. Hundreds of volunteer tutors were trained to teach and witness to persons learning English as a second language. As we became preoccupied with this volunteer work, one account after another of visions would fall into our hands, and, being led by the Holy Spirit, we were determined and inspired to continue the compilation. We earnestly pray that this effort might bring glory to our Lord and might lead souls to Him.

Lucile Huyssen

VISIONS OF JESUS

SEVENTEEN
BIBLICAL
VISIONS
OF CHRIST

Abraham Sees the Word

After these things the word of the Lord came unto Abram in a vision, saying, Fear not, Abram: I am thy shield, and thy exceeding great reward . . . .

Genesis 15:1

* * * * *

The Prophet Micaiah

And he said, Hear thou therefore the word of the Lord: I saw the Lord sitting on his throne, and all the host of heaven standing by him on his right hand and on his left.

1 Kings 22:19

* * * * *

The Prophet Isaiah

In the year that King Uzziah died I saw also the Lord sitting upon a throne, high and lifted up, and his train filled the temple. Above it stood the seraphims: each one had six wings; with twain he covered his face, and with twain he covered his feet, and with twain he did fly. And one cried unto another and said, Holy, holy, holy is the Lord of hosts: the whole earth is full of his glory. And the posts of the door moved at the voice of him that cried, and the house was filled with smoke.

Then said I, Woe is me! for I am undone; because I am a man of unclean lips, and I dwell in the midst of a people of unclean lips: for mine eyes have seen the King, the Lord of hosts.

Isaiah 6:1-5

* * * * *

The Prophet Ezekiel

By the River Chebar

Now it came to pass in the thirtieth year, in the fourth month, in the fifth day of the month, as I was among the captives by the river of Chebar, that the heavens were opened, and I saw visions of God. In the fifth day of the month, which was the fifth year of King Jehoiachin's captivity, the word of the Lord came expressly unto Ezekiel the priest, the son of Buzi, in the land of the Chaldeans by the river Chebar; and the hand of the Lord was there upon him.

Ezekiel 1:1-3

Visions of the Lord and Jerusalem

And it came to pass in the sixth year, in the sixth month, in the fifth day of the month, as I sat in mine house, and the elders of Judah sat before me, that the hand of the Lord God fell there upon me. Then I beheld, and lo a likeness as the appearance of fire: from the appearance of his loins even downward, fire; and his loins even upward, as the appearance of brightness, as the colour of amber. And he put forth the form of a hand, and took me by a lock of mine head; and the spirit lifted me up between the earth and heaven, and brought me in the visions of God to Jerusalem, to the door of the inner gate that looketh toward the north; where was the seat of the image of jealousy, which provoketh to jealousy. And, behold, the glory of the God of Israel was there, according to the vision that I saw in the plain. *Ezekiel 8:1-4*

The Glory of the God of Israel

Afterward he brought me to the gate, even the gate that looketh toward the east: And, behold, the glory of the God of Israel came from the way of the east: and his voice was like a noise of many waters: and the earth shined with his glory. And it was according to the appearance of the vision which I saw, even according to the vision that I saw when I came to destroy the city: and the visions were like the vision that I saw by the river Chebar; and I fell upon my face. And the glory of the Lord came into the house by the way of the gate whose prospect is toward the east. So the spirit took me up, and brought me into the inner court; and, behold, the glory of the Lord filled the house. And I heard him speaking unto me out of the house; and the man stood by me.

Ezekiel 43:1-6

* * * * *

The Prophet Daniel

And in the four and twentieth day of the first month, as I was by the side of the great river, which is Hiddekel; Then I lifted up mine eyes, and looked, and behold a certain man clothed in linen, whose loins were girded with fine gold of Uphaz: His body also was like the beryl, and his face as the appearance of lightning, and his eyes as lamps of fire, and his arms and his feet like in colour to polished brass, and the voice of his words like the voice of a multitude. And I Daniel alone saw the vision: for the men that were with me saw not the vision; but a great quaking fell upon them, so that they fled to hide themselves. Therefore I was left alone, and saw this great vision, and there remained no strength in me: for my comeliness was turned in me into corruption, and I retained no strength. Yet heard I the voice of his words: and when I heard the voice of his words, then was I in a deep sleep on my face, and my face toward the ground.

And, behold, an hand touched me, which set me upon my knees and upon the palms of my hands. And he said unto me, O Daniel, a man greatly beloved, understand the words that I speak unto thee, and stand upright: for unto thee am I now sent. And when he had spoken this word unto me, I stood trembling. Then said he unto me, Fear not, Daniel: for from the first day that thou didst set thine heart to understand, and to chasten thyself before thy God, thy words were heard, and I am come for thy words.

Daniel 10:4-12

Jesus Transfigured

And after six days Jesus taketh Peter, James, and John his brother, and bringeth them up into a high mountain apart, And was transfigured before them: and his face did shine as the sun, and his raiment was white as the light. And, behold, there appeared unto them Moses and Elias talking with him. Then answered Peter, and said unto Jesus, Lord, it is good for us to be here: if thou wilt, let us make here three tabernacles; one for thee, and one for Moses, and one for Elias. While he yet spake, behold, a bright cloud overshadowed them: and behold a voice out of the cloud, which said, This is my beloved Son, in whom I am well pleased; hear ye him. And when the disciples heard it, they fell on their face, and were sore afraid. And Jesus came and touched them, and said, Arise, and be not afraid. And when they had lifted up their eyes, they saw no man, save Jesus only. And as they came down from the mountain, Jesus charged them, saying, Tell the vision to no man, until the Son of man be risen again from the dead.

Matthew 17:1-9

Stephen Beholds the Glorified Son of Man

When they heard these things, they were cut to the heart, and they gnashed on him with their teeth. But he, being full of the Holy Ghost, looked up steadfastly into heaven, and saw the glory of God, and Jesus standing on the right hand of God, And said, Behold, I see the heavens opened, and the Son of man standing on the right hand of God. Then they cried out with a loud voice, and stopped their ears, and ran upon him with one accord, And cast him out of the city, and

6

stoned him: and the witnesses laid down their clothes at a young man's feet, whose name was Saul.

Acts 7:54-58

* * * * *

Saul, on the Road to Damascus

And Saul, yet breathing out threatenings and slaughter against the disciples of the Lord, went unto the high priest, And desired of him letters to Damascus to the synagogues, that if he found any of this way, whether they were men or women, he might bring them bound unto Jerusalem. And as he journeyed, he came near Damascus: and suddenly there shined round about him a light from heaven: And he fell to the earth, and heard a voice saying unto him, Saul, Saul, why persecutest thou me? And he said, Who art thou, Lord? And the Lord said, I am Jesus whom thou persecutest: it is hard for thee to kick against the pricks. And he trembling and astonished said, Lord, what wilt thou have me to do? And the Lord said unto him, Arise, and go into the city, and it shall be told thee what thou must do. And the men which journeyed with him stood speechless, hearing a voice, but seeing no man. And Saul arose from the earth; and when his eyes were opened, he saw no man: but they led him by the hand, and brought him into Damascus. And he was three days without sight, and neither did eat nor drink.

Acts 9:1-9

* * * * *

The Lord Visits Ananias

And there was a certain disciple at Damascus, named Ananias; and to him said the Lord in a vision, Ananias. And he said, Behold, I am here, Lord. And the Lord said unto him, Arise, and go into the street which is called Straight, and inquire in the house of Judas for one called Saul, of Tarsus:

7

for, behold, he prayeth, And hath seen in a vision a man named Ananias coming in, and putting his hand on him, that he might receive his sight. Then Ananias answered, Lord, I have heard by many of this man, how much evil he hath done to thy saints at Jerusalem: And here he hath authority from the chief priests to bind all that call on thy name. But the Lord said unto him, Go thy way: for he is a chosen vessel unto me, to bear my name before the Gentiles, and kings, and the children of Israel: For I will show him how great things he must suffer for my name's sake.

And Ananias went his way, and entered into the house; and putting his hands on him said, Brother Saul, the Lord, even Jesus, that appeared unto thee in the way as thou camest, hath sent me, that thou mightest receive thy sight, and be filled with the Holy Ghost. And immediately there fell from his eyes as it had been scales: and he received sight forthwith, and arose, and was baptized. And when he had received meat, he was strengthened. Then was Saul certain days with the disciples which were at Damascus.

Acts 9:10-19

* * * * *

Jesus Speaks to Paul at Corinth
Then spake the Lord to Paul in the night by a vision, Be not afraid, but speak, and hold not thy peace: For I am with thee, and no man shall set on thee to hurt thee: for I have much people in this city. And he continued there a year and six months, teaching the word of God among them.

Acts 18:9-11

* * * * *

Warned in Jerusalem
And it came to pass, that, when I was come again to Jerusalem, even while I prayed in the temple, I was in a

trance; And saw him saying unto me, Make haste, and get thee quickly out of Jerusalem: for they will not receive thy testimony concerning me. And I said, Lord, they know that I imprisoned and beat in every synagogue them that believed on thee: And when the blood of thy martyr Stephen was shed, I also was standing by, and consenting unto his death, and kept the raiment of them that slew him. And he said unto me, Depart: for I will send thee far hence unto the Gentiles.

Acts 22:17-21

* * * * *

Paul Comforted at Jerusalem

And the night following the Lord stood by him, and said, Be of good cheer, Paul: for as thou hast testified of me in Jerusalem, so must thou bear witness also at Rome.

Acts 23:11

* * * * *

John on the Island of Patmos

I was in the Spirit on the Lord's day, and heard behind me a great voice, as of a trumpet, Saying, I am Alpha and Omega, the first and the last: and, What thou seest, write in a book, and send it unto the seven churches which are in Asia; unto Ephesus, and unto Smyrna, and unto Pergamos, and unto Thyatira, and unto Sardis, and unto Philadelphia, and unto Laodicea. And I turned to see the voice that spake with me. And being turned, I saw seven golden candlesticks; And in the midst of the seven candlesticks one like unto the Son of man, clothed with a garment down to the foot, and girt about the paps with a golden girdle. His head and his hairs were white like wool, as white as snow; and his eyes were as a flame of fire; And his feet like unto fine brass, as if they burned in a furnace; and his voice as the sound of many waters. And he had in his right hand seven stars: and out of his mouth went a sharp two-edged sword: and his countenance was as the sun shineth in his strength. And when

9

I saw him, I fell at his feet as dead. And he laid his right hand upon me, saying unto me, Fear not: I am the first and the last: I am he that liveth, and was dead; and, behold, I am alive for evermore, Amen; and have the keys of hell and of death. Write the things which thou hast seen, and the things which are, and the things which shall be hereafter; The mystery of the seven stars which thou sawest in my right hand, and the seven golden candlesticks. The seven stars are the angels of the seven churches: and the seven candlesticks which thou sawest are the seven churches.

Revelation 1:10-20

* * * * *

John Sees the Majesty of God

After this I looked, and, behold, a door was opened in heaven: and the first voice which I heard was as it were of a trumpet talking with me: which said, Come up hither, and I will show thee things which must be hereafter. And immediately I was in the spirit: and, behold, a throne was set in heaven, and one sat on the throne. And he that sat was to look upon like a jasper and a sardine stone: and there was a rainbow round about the throne, in sight like unto an emerald.

Revelation 4:1-3

* * * * *

John Hears the New Song

And I looked, and, lo, a Lamb stood on the mount Sion, and with him a hundred forty and four thousand, having his Father's name written in their foreheads. And I heard a voice from heaven, as the voice of many waters, and as the voice of a great thunder: and I heard the voice of harpers harping with their harps: And they sung as it were a new song before the throne, and before the four beasts, and the elders: and no man could learn that song but the hundred and forty and four thousand, which were redeemed from the earth.

Revelation 14:1-3

ANCIENT
AND
MEDIEVAL
SAINTS

Saint Anthony

We read that St. Anthony once suffered greatly in the desert of evil spirits and that when he had overcome his difficulty, our Lord appeared, visible and joyous.

Then the saint said: "Ah, Lord, where were you just now when I needed you so much?"

Our Lord replied: "I was here just as I am now but I did want the pleasure of seeing how staunch a person you are." Silver and gold may be pure, but when it comes to making a cup from which a king is to drink, it is burnt far longer than for other purposes.

Thus the apostles wrote that they rejoiced at being worthy to suffer contempt and misery for God.

Reprinted with permission of Harper and Row Publishers, Inc., New York, from *Meister Eckhart*, a modern translation by Raymond B. Blacknew. Copyright 1941.

* * * * *

Saint Francis of Assisi

It was on the feast of the Exaltation of the Holy Cross, tradition tells us, that the supreme event of this retreat and of the life of Saint Francis took place. At dawn that morning, Francis, kneeling on the advanced spur of rock which fell away below him for thousands of feet and facing the east where the first light of the sun was breaking, prayed to God for two favors. The first was that before he died, he should feel in his body, as far as might be possible, the actual sufferings of Christ's Passions; and the second was that he might feel the very love which had caused Christ to undergo this sacrifice for mankind.

When this prayer was ended, we are told, a seraph with six wings flew down toward him, and as it approached, the image of a man on a cross appeared between the pairs of wings. It was the figure of Christ, Himself, and as it rested in front of the Saint, darts of flame imprinted on Francis's body the wounds of the crucified Christ. His hands and his feet were pierced with the nails, and on his right side was the wound of the lance. His pilgrimage had stretched from the crucifix of San Damiamo to this mystic crucifixion of his own spirit and body.

For the rest of his life, Francis carried on his body the stigmata: the round, blackened nail-head scars on his hands and on his feet, and the lance wound from which at times blood flowed in sufficient quantity, in some cases to penetrate through his clothes.

We have Celano's testimony in regard to the nature of these mysterious wounds. "Hands and feet were pierced in the center by nails, the head of which could be seen in the palm of the hand and in the upper side of the feet. The points of these nails came out on the opposite sides; the marks in the palm of the hand were rounded; and, on the back of the hands, they were long, and there appeared a little bit of flesh just like a bent and driven back point of a nail, coming through beyond the flesh. So also with the feet. The marks of the nails were impressed and the mark showed up above the rest of the flesh. It was as though the right side had been pierced by a lance, with a long wound which often spouted out blood which on many an occasion seeped through the tunic and undergarments.

Few people indeed were able to see the sacred wounds of the side while the crucified son of the crucified Lord was alive, but how lucky was Elias who even during the Saint's lifetime, managed to see it. Lucky, too, Rufino who actually touched it with his own hands.

On one occasion Rufino had to touch the Saint's chest in order to rub it, and slipped, as often happens, right over to the right side. In doing so he touched the precious wound and the Saint as a result felt great pain so much so that he pushed Rufino's hand away saying, 'May God forgive you!' The fact was that he always did everything he could to hide this prodigy from strangers and kept it as quiet as he possibly

14

could even from his friends. The result was that even the most intimate and fervent of his brothers knew nothing about it for a long time.''

*   *   *   *   *

Blessed Aleyde

In the middle of the thirteenth century Sister Aleyde entered the Convent of La Cambre, near Brussels, at the age of seven. After years of devoted service in the convent, Aleyde became ill and the physician told the little nun that she had leprosy and would have to live in a cell.

Aleyde was keyed up by the announcement that she was a leper, and hence was keener in her perception than usual. She saw the fear in the eyes of all, she noted the shrinking away of even the bravest and efforts of others to avoid her very presence. She was somewhat bewildered by it all but tried to be as kind and generous in her thoughts as she could be. But she was human enough to feel hurt by the actions of the frightened ones and the attitude of the truly timid. . . .

The cell was built. The little nun was led to it. She entered with a smile on her somewhat distorted face and she kept her promise: she was not afraid. And the Christ who could not resist the faith of the leper who prostrated himself saying: "Lord, if Thou wilt . . .'' nor the plea of those who cried, "Master, mercy . . .'' was so touched by this trust of the tiny Belgian nun that He appeared to her, smiled, and said: "Aleyde, you will never want. I shall be your Cellarer.'' When we realize that the cellarer, according to St. Benedict's Rule, is he who provides everything the brethren may need, we can see why the little leper knew she had received something better than a cure. . . .

Aleyde had insisted that she be awakened at midnight so that she might assist at the Resurrection. The heroic attendant agreed and, after arousing her, helped her to a prie-dieu. Through the open windows of the church and into the tiny cell came the happy chant of the Easter Alleluias. The Office moved on and the lessons were being sung when the attendant noticed the little leper shift her position on the prie-dieu. This was exceptional, for Aleyde's knees were so sick and sore that any movement was excruciating. Suddenly the chant of the responsory Surrexit Dominus de sepulchro . . . was begun. Aleyde's eyes, sunk deep in dark sockets, and looking like pools of fire, seemed to open wider and wider. The attendant followed their gaze and saw the sky above them open like some great curtain, while light, as from the face of some fiery furnace, sprouted down upon the convent, setting every building brilliantly aglow. The Sister attendant cried out in fright. Aleyde made a quiet gesture with what remained of her right hand which told the nun not to be scared. Then the tiny cell drank in, as it were, the torrent of celestial light, and the truth that the mystery the responsory told about was being re-enacted became plain to the Sister attendant. Christ, the Risen and Glorified, had come to visit the soul of one who was as white as snow not only physically, but also spiritually.

As Easter Week moved on Aleyde's state became more and more agonizing. Once when the pain squeezed a cry from her the attendant was moved to such pity that she spoke of the words Aleyde had used the first day they dwelt together.

"Sister," she said, 'I have often heard you lament the length of your exile. I know your longing for heaven. I also know something of the agonies you endure. Tell me, please, that what you said to me the first day I came to you is not true. Tell me that you will not live after me; that you will not suffer much more.''

Aleyde looked her gratitude for such genuine sympathy but made no reply. It was only later in the day that she turned to the Sister and said: "Sister dear, what I told you that first day is true. You will die before me, and you will go straight to God. You must then help me even more than you do now; for Jesus has told me that the sufferings of these past years are as nothing compared to what I will yet suffer."

"Oh!" cried the attendant. "How can that be! How could God ask so much! Oh, Sister!"

Aleyde's sunken eyes lit with that smile which could not brighten any other feature but her eyes, so far had the leprosy progressed.

"And you can smile at such a prospect!" exclaimed the attendant.

"It is a happiness," replied the leper. "It is a great happiness to help God. Jesus has told me that there are certain souls that cannot be saved—cannot be saved, mind you—unless I suffer. That is why I am glad to remain here after you have gone. That is why I am happy that this body of mine can serve the Christ. But never forget what I said. You must help me from heaven. I do not like pain!"

Reprinted from "Blessed Aleyde," *These Women Walked with God*, by Reverend M. Raymond, OCSO, published by Benziger, Bruce and Glencoe, Inc. (previously Bruce Publishing Company), Milwaukee, Wisconsin, copyright © 1956.

* * * * *

Saint Germanus

Saint Germanus, also known as Saint Germain, was a French ecclesiastic of the fifth century. He became the bishop of Auxerre in 418. In 429 he went to Britain and successfully argued against the Pelagian heresy, which denied original sin and maintained the freedom of the will. He visited Britain again in 447 and succeeded in defeating the Pelagians once more. He died in 448.

17

While they were returning from his place, the very watchful Devil contrived that Germanus should fall and break a leg, not knowing that, like blessed Job, his merits would be enhanced by bodily affliction. While he was thus detained by illness, fire broke out in a cottage near his lodging, and after destroying the adjoining dwellings which were thatched with reeds, it was carried by the wind to the cottage where he lay. The people ran to pick up the bishop and carry him to a place of safety, but full of trust in God, he reproved them and would not allow them to do so. In despair, the people ran off to fight the fire, but to afford clearer evidence of God's power, whatever the crowd endeavoured to save was destroyed. Meanwhile the flames leaped over the house where the saint lay disabled and helpless, but although they raged all around it, the place that sheltered him stood untouched amid a sea of fire. The crowd was overjoyed at the miracle, and praised God for this proof of His power, while innumerable poor folk kept vigil outside his cottage day and night hoping for healing of soul or body.

It is impossible to relate all that Christ effected through his servant, and what wonders the sick saint performed. And while he refused any treatment for his own illness, he saw beside him one night a being in shining robes, who seemed to reach out his hand and raise him up, ordering him to stand on his feet. From that moment his pain ceased, his former health was restored, and when dawn came, he continued on his journey undaunted.

Reprinted with permission of Penguin Books Limited, London, from Bede's *A History of the English Church and People,* translated by Leo Sherley-Price. Copyright 1955, Leo Sherley-Price.

* * * * *

Archbishop Cyprian

Thacius Cecilius Cyprianus was born near Carthage in Africa. His father was a wealthy Roman officer of high rank. Cyprian was given a good Greek education. He became a man of commanding literary and rhetorical culture, and eminent in administrative ability. In middle life he became a Christian. He led a retired penitential life and within less than a year he was compelled to succeed Donatus as Bishop of Carthage. The following year Decius became Emperor and a bloody persecution broke out. St. Cyprian felt it wise to leave Carthage for a while though he kept in touch with his flock. He was martyred about 258, during the persecution by Valerian.

Many clerics and laymen had forgotten that they were purchased by the blood of Christ not to be like other people but to be different, to be the salt of the earth and to consider themselves blessed "when men shall hate you, and when they shall reject you and revile you and ban your name as evil, for the Son of man's sake," but "woe to you who are rich . . . woe to you when all men speak well of you!" (Luke 6:22-26). Evidently some harsh blow was needed from time to time to call the children of light back from flesh pots to spiritual realities. One of them was about to fall on the flock of the new archbishop of Carthage.

It came about in 249 with the elevation of Caius Messius Quintus Trajanus Decius to the imperial purple. This mediocre soldier and capable administrator believed that the destructive and centrifugal forces at work in the Empire could be checked and reversed by reorganization. Rightly discerning a connection between religion and morality, he wrongly concluded that the way to restore the moral vigor and health of Roman life was to return to the worship of the ancient gods . . . All lay Christians must prove their loyalty to the state cult by sacrificing two grains of incense to the gods, or pay the penalty of death.

After all, what were two grains of incense?

The blow fell so suddenly that large masses of lax and compromising Christians were unable to sustain it. Thousands, to be sure, stood firm and joined their bishops and priests in enduring the cruelest tortures and the most excruciating deaths rather than deny Christ. Other thousands fled to the mountains and to the deserts, to live in huts and caves until the storm blew over—especially in Egypt, where the persecution of Decius brought about results, as we shall see, very different from his expectations. But the saddest chapter was written by those thousands who either worshiped the idols or pretended to do so to save their lives. For every martyr and refugee there was probably one of these miserable apostates.

When the edict of Decius reached Carthage at the beginning of 250, there were very similiar results. Many fled to the mountains or the desert, but many others hastened to sacrifice, to burn incense or to buy certificates.

Cyprian as usual had recourse to prayer. Should he wait for his arrest by the imperial troops or go forth boldly and offer himself up? According to his own account he had a vision in which the Lord told him to depart from the city and hide himself in the desert until the storm spent itself. If he was killed now, there would be no one to reorganize and reform the Catholics of Carthage, and the Faith might vanish from Africa. And had not Jesus Himself fled from His persecutors more than once, because His time had not yet come? Cyprian arose from his knees and stole away.

From *Saints in Action* by William Thomas Walsh. Copyright © 1961 by Doubleday and Company, Inc. Used by permission of publisher.

TESTIMONIES
PRIOR TO THE
TWENTIETH
CENTURY

From The Journal of John Wesley

John Wesley, founder of Methodism, was born at Epworth Rectory, June 17, 1703. He was the fifteenth child of the Rev. Samuel's nineteen children. In 1738 Wesley found great faith at a meeting in Aldersgate Street, in London, where, "I found my heart strangely warmed. I felt I did trust in Christ, Christ alone, for salvation; and an assurance was given me that He had taken away my sins, even mine, and saved me from the law of sin and death." Wesley generally travelled about fifty thousand miles a year. He is said to have delivered more than four thousand sermons.

MONDAY 6th (Everton) — I talked largely with Ann Thorne and two others, who had been several times in trances. What they all agreed in was 1) that when they went away, as they termed it, it was always at the time they were fullest of the love of God; 2) that it came upon them in a moment, without any previous notice, and took away all their senses and strength; 3) that there were some exceptions, but in general, from that moment, they were in another world, knowing nothing of what was done or said by all that were around them.

"About five in the afternoon I heard them singing hymns. Soon after, Mr. Bee came up and told me Alice Miller (15 years old) had fallen into a trance . . . I do not know whether I ever saw a human face look so beautiful; sometimes it was covered with a smile, as from joy, mixing with love and reverence; but the tears fell still while not so fast. Her pulse was quite regular. In about a half an hour I observed her countenance change into the form of fear, pity, and distress; then she burst into a flood of tears and cried out, 'Dear Lord; they will be damned!' But in about five minutes her smiles returned, and only love and joy appeared in her face.

" . . . About seven her senses returned. I asked, 'Where have you been?'

" 'Where have you been?'

" 'I have been with my Saviour.' "
" 'In heaven or on earth?' "
" 'I cannot tell; but I was in glory.' "

*   *   *   *   *

The Sexton's Strange Apparition
From *The Journal of John Wesley*

SATURDAY, August 1. — Before I left Glasgow I heard so strange an account that I desired to hear it from the person himself. He was a sexton and yet for many years had little troubled himself about religion. I set down his words and leave every man to form his own judgment upon them: "Sixteen weeks ago, I was walking, an hour before sunset, behind the high kirk; and, looking on one side, I saw one close to me who looked in my face and asked me how I did. I answered, 'Pretty well.' He said, 'You have had many troubles; but how have you improved them?' He then told me all that ever I did; yea, and the thoughts that had been in my heart; adding, 'Be ready for my second coming'; and he was gone I knew not how. I trembled all over, and had no strength in me; but sank down to the ground. From that time I groaned continually under the load of sin, till at the Lord's supper it was all taken away."

Used by permission of Moody Press.

*   *   *   *   *

A. Alice Miller

I knew a man in Christ above fourteen years ago (whether in the body, I cannot tell; or whether out of the body, I cannot tell: God knoweth); such an one caught up to the third heaven. And I knew such a man (whether in the body, or out of the body, I cannot tell: God knoweth); How that he was caught up in to paradise, and heard uspeakable works, which it is not lawful for a man to utter.

2 Corinthians 12:2-4

B. The Sexton's Strange Apparition

And he took the cup, and gave thanks, and gave it to them, saying, Drink ye all of it; For this is my blood of the new testament, which is shed for many for the remission of sins.

Matthew 26: 27,28

For the Lord himself shall descend from heaven with a shout, with the voice of the archangel, and with the trump of God: and the dead in Christ shall rise first: Then we which are alive and remain shall be caughtup together with them in the clouds, to meet the Lord in the air: and so shall we ever be with the Lord.

1 Thessalonians 4:16,17

*   *   *   *   *

A Vision of Jesus
by Charles G. Finney

This account of Charles G. Finney's initial experience with God is one of the most remarkable accounts of the Holy Spirit's power since the days of the apostles. During the year 1857-58, the Lord guided him in winning over one hundred thousand persons to Christ. The Holy Spirit so impressed the conscience of men with the necessity of holy living in such a way as to obtain lasting results. Research shows that 85% of his converts remained true to God.

I went to my dinner, and found I had no appetite to eat. I then went to the office. My mind remained in that profoundly tranquil state. There was a great sweetness and tenderness in my thoughts and feelings. Everything appeared to be going right, and nothing seemed to ruffle or disturb me in the least. My heart seemed to be liquid within me. All my feelings seemed to rise and flow out; and the utterance of my heart was, "I want to pour my whole soul out to God." The rising of my soul was so great that I rushed into the room back of the front office, to pray. There was no fire, and no light, in the room; nevertheless it appeared to me as if it were perfectly light. As I went in and shut the door after me, it seemed as if I met the Lord Jesus Christ face to face. It did not occur to me then, nor did it for some time afterward, that it was wholly a mental state.

On the contrary, it seemed to me that I saw Him as I would see any other man. He said nothing, but looked at me in such a manner as to break me right down at His feet. I have always since regarded this as a most remarkable state of mind; for it seemed to me a reality, that He stood before me, and I fell down at His feet and poured out my soul to Him. I wept aloud like a child, and made such confessions as I could with my choked utterance. It seemed to me that I bathed His feet with my tears; and yet I had no distinct impression that I touched Him, that I recollect.

Used by permission of Free Gospel Society

And when the centurion, which stood over against him, saw that he so cried out, and gave up the ghost, he said, Truly this man was the Son of God.

Mark 15:39

* * * * *

Sundar Singh's Vision
Sadhu Sundar Singh (1889-1929) was probably the most Christ-like saint of the last century. Having forsaken wealth, fame, and family for Jesus' sake, he became extremely popular among Christians but was persecuted by others in his country. He was well received in many other countries throughout the world.

Though, according to my ideas at that time, I thought I had

done a good deed in burning the Gospel, yet my unrest of heart increased, and for two days after that I was very miserable. On the third day, when I felt I could bear it no longer, I got up at three in the morning, and after bathing, I prayed that if there was a God at all He would reveal Himself to me, and show me the way of salvation, and end this unrest of my soul. I firmly made up my mind that, if this prayer was not answered, I would before daylight go down to the railway and place my head on the line before the oncoming train. I remained till about half-past four, praying and waiting and expecting to see Krishna, or Buddha, or some other Avatar of the Hindu religion, but they appeared not, but a light shone in the room. I opened the door to see where it came from, but all was dark outside. I returned inside, and the light increased in intensity and took the form of a globe of light above the ground and in this light there appeared, not the form I expected, but the Living Christ whom I had counted as dead. To all eternity I shall never forget His glorious and loving face, nor the few words which He spoke, "Why do you persecute me? See, I have died on the cross for you and for the whole world." These words were burned into my heart as by lightning, and I fell on the ground before Him. My heart was filled with inexpressible joy and peace, and my whole life was entirely changed.

Reprinted by permission from *Reverse Side of the Cross*, by Rufus Moseley, copyright 1952 by Macalester Park Publishing Company, St. Paul, Minnesota.

While he yet spake, behold, a bright cloud overshadowed them: and behold a voice out of the cloud, which said, This is my beloved Son, in whom I am well pleased; hear ye him.

Matthew 17:5

Jesus saith unto him, I am the way, the truth, and the life: no man cometh unto the Father, but by me.

John 14:6

For I delivered unto you first of all that which I also received, how that Christ died for our sins according to the scriptures; And that he was buried, and that he rose again the third day according to the scriptures.

1 Corinthians 15:3,4

* * * * *

Marietta Davis: An Angelic Trip with Jesus

H.A. Baker, missionary to Tibet, China, and Formosa, is author of The Three Worlds, Visions Beyond the Veil, Plains of Glory and Gloom, Heaven and Angels, *and other books; he records the following incident:*

For nine days, Marietta Davis, free from any sickness, lay in a state of trance from which she could not be awakened. During that time in vision she was caught up to heaven to see conditions in the Infant Paradise. She also saw in part other sections of heaven as well as parts of hell. Her book, Scenes Beyond the Grave, *was written one hundred years ago.*

Judging from the especially revealed order on the plain in the city of the Infant Paradise, the place where infants are first nurtured and trained, we get marvelously illuminating insight into the perfect system of angelic ministry in heaven. Marietta Davis was led to heaven to receive particularly an insight into the plan of ministry among infants. By Jesus Himself she was told to make things known on earth. She was given comprehensive insight into the angelic ministry in one of the infant homes of the lowest order.

One angel of high rank presided over that home. Its face and body radiated the brightest light, the manifestation that is in proportion to rank and power. Working harmoniously with this head angel were seven others somewhat less in power and radiant light and life. Each of these seven, in turn, had loving charge of seven other angels somewhat lower in power and radiance.

Each angel in this lower rank was in charge of a class of "guardian angels" each of whom nurtured and developed the unfolding life of an infant in her charge. In this one home fifty-six angels gladly obeyed directions from angels of higher rank as they served those of lower order than themselves. . . . Angels returning from earth and bringing in their arms infants who had just died, upon reaching the infants' home in Paradise, gave over the children to other angels in the home whose duty it was to care for the new arrivals. The infants in the charge of these guardian angels were later passed on to more advanced homes on the same infant plain and so on until at last they reached the great central home on this plain. From there, in time, these children were advanced to begin again in the outer, or lower, grade of the next higher plain, and then from home to home and plain to plain, "from glory to glory," as we have already shown.

It can be seen at once that all this angelic order is in accord with the principles of God. He is a "God of order." His system is so perfect that not a sparrow falls without His notice.

From Heaven and the Angels by H. A. Baker, published by Osterbus Publishing House, Minneapolis, Minnesota.

In my Father's house are many mansions: if it were not so, I would have told you. I go to prepare a place for you.

John 14:2

*　*　*　*　*

TESTIMONIES OF THE TWENTIETH CENTURY

General Booth of the
Salvation Army

William Booth (1829-1912) was the founder and leader of the Salvation Army. He was born of Church of England parents in England. When William was about thirteen his father died leaving him and his mother in poverty, which meant he could not secure even a good common school education. While still young he was converted in a little Methodist chapel and became interested in mission work and evangelistic preaching.

In his mission work he met Catherine Mumford of London and later married her. Catherine became an ideal co-worker with him in his great work in the Salvation Army.

In 1865 William Booth began doing missionary work and preaching to the poor in East London. This is where the Salvation Army had its beginnings, first as the "East London Christian Revival Society." Later, in 1878 the society was organized with military form, name, and discipline, calling it the Salvation Army. His organization continued to be devoted to practical philanthropy as well as street preaching and personal evangelism. In 1890 he published his great book, In Darkest England On The Way Out.

General Booth was allowed to see some of the marshalled hosts of heaven, and he says:

"What a sight that was! Worth toiling a lifetime to behold it! Nearest the King were the patriarchs and apostles of ancient time. Next, rank after rank, came the holy martyrs who had died for Him. Then came the army of warriors who had fought for Him in every part of the world; and around and about, above and below, I beheld myriads of spirits who were never heard of outside their own neighborhoods, or beyond their own times, who with self-denying zeal and untiring toil had labored to extend God's kingdom and to save souls of men.

"Encircling this gorgeous scene above, beneath, around,

hovered glittering angelic beings who had kept their first estate, proud, it seemed to me, to minister to the happiness and exaltation of those redeemed out of the poor world whence I came.

"I was bewildered by the scene. The songs, the music, the shouts of the multitude came like the roar of a thousand cataracts, echoed and re-echoed through the glory-lit mountains, and the magnificent and endless army of happy spirits ravished my senses with passionate delight."

Then the King addressed General Booth who, until that time, had lived a nominal, useless, lazy, professing Christian life, and said:

"Thou wilt feel thyself little in harmony with these, once the companions of my tribulation and now of my glory, who counted not their lives dear unto themselves in order to bring honor to me and salvation to me." And he gave a look of admiration at the host of apostles and martyrs and warriors gathered around Him.

"Oh, that look of Jesus! I felt that to have one such loving recognition would be worth dying a hundred deaths at the stake, worth being torn asunder by wild beasts. The angelic escort felt it, too, for their responsive burst of praise shook the very skies and the ground on which I lay.

"Then the King turned His eyes on me again. How I wished that some mountain would fall upon me and hide me forever from His presence! But I wished in vain. Some invisible and irresistible force compelled me to look up, and my eyes met His once more. I felt, rather than heard, Him saying to me in words that engaged themselves as fire upon my brain: 'Go back to earth. I will give you another opportunity. Prove thyself worthy of my name. Show to the world that thou possessest my Spirit by doing my work and becoming, on my behalf, a saviour of men.

" 'Thou shalt return hither [to heaven] when thou hast finished the battle, and I will give thee a place in my conquering train and a share in my glory.' "

When the Lord led General Booth and others to heaven to see the glory and exalted state of those who suffer most for Jesus and endure most for Him in saving men, it was not for the good of those heavenly visitors only, but for us as well. The Lord wants it made known to all His people that the highest privilege of man is to humble himself low and suffer much for Jesus' sake and man's salvation.

After this magnificent experience, General Booth became deeply concerned about the poverty of the lower classes in England and he devoted himself to the poor and homeless.

He was founder and first General of the Salvation Army. An early street-corner preacher and later an ordained Methodist New Connexion minister, he preached, averaging two sermons a day, almost until the time of his death.

From *Heaven and the Angels* by H. A. Baker, Osterbus Publishing House, Minneapolis, Minnesota.

Therefore said he unto them, The harvest truly is great, but the labourers are few: pray ye therefore the Lord of the harvest, that he would send forth labourers into his harvest.

Luke 10:2

And he said to them all, If any man will come after me, let him deny himself, and take up his cross daily, and follow me. For whosoever will save his life shall lose it: but whosoever will lose his life for my sake, the same shall save it. For what is a man advantaged, if he gain the whole world, and lose himself, or be cast away? For whosoever shall be ashamed of me and of my words, of him shall the Son of man be ashamed, when he shall come in his own glory, and in his Father's and of the holy angels.

Luke 9:23-26

If any man serve me, let him follow me; and where I am, there shall also my servant be: if any man serve me, him will my Father honour.

John 12:26

J. Rufus Moseley

J. Rufus Moseley is the author of Manifest Victory, Perfect Everything *and* The Reverse Side of the Cross. *He lived a deeply religious life.*

In the following excerpt from Manifest Victory, *Mr. Moseley gives a genuine, exact account of his own vision of Christ and also relates accounts of his friends and acquaintances who had had visions of our Lord.*

"The power, the control, the wonder of the singing upon my lips and the music upon my whole body, increased and the Presence moved upon and within me and by my happy consent and yielding lifted me as on the cross. My arms were outstretched and my whole body perfectly upright. In this position I became aware of a glorious Presence standing immediately before me in the tangible form of a man, imparting the sense of barely concealed powers and immense sanctity. He made Himself known as Jesus and infused Himself within me. The way He came was the reverse of the way human personalities leave the body with the going of the breath.

"I fell upon my face at His feet, as one dead and yet more alive than I dreamed it possible to ever be. I knew at once that He was in me and I in Him, as the Father was in Him and He in the Father.

"That which occurred in my experience was like the occurrence, according to scriptural record, on the first night after His resurrection, when Jesus stood among the eleven and said to them, 'Peace be unto you, as my Father has sent Me, even so I send you.' And when He had said this, He breathed on them and said unto them, 'Receive ye the Holy Ghost.'

"The first day I was at Dr. Allen's, Sunday, March 27,

1910, I fell into such a deep sleep that it was hard to awaken me. When awakened I saw Jesus in the face of the kind servant sent to awaken me. I was in such a realm of glory that I was not certain whether I had been awakened from profound human sleep, or resurrected death. Everything had a halo of light and glory around it. Even the cattle and the chickens, to use a fine line of Browning's, 'had learned the new law,' so surpassing were they in form, movement, grace, and beauty.

"During the year 1926, I did the hardest physical work of my whole life; I also did some of my best writing. Best of all, it was during this year that Jesus gave me visions of Himself as glorified man and also gave increasingly the keys of abiding union with Him.

"After my return to Macon, a friend complained of chills and fever and that the chills came upon her at regular times. I told her about the healing of the woman in St. Louis and the Lord Himself appeared to make known to her that any one believing in Him should not be hurt by the germs of malaria. She rejoiced and said she had the assurance that she would not have another chill; she did not. She was set free from malaria at that very moment.

"As I was standing and talking with my external eyes closed, I was granted visions of the face of Jesus. The face as shown me was that of perfect, glorified, universal man. He looked as I feel Plato might have conceived the ideal human archetype—but glorified through union with Jesus. Jesus, of course, has the power to appear in any form that is most helpful.

"The Second Baptist Church of Saint Louis, as well as the wonderful Catholic Cathedral, were kept open so that one could enter for meditation and prayer. In both I had precious manifestations of His presence.

37

"Another friend, Mrs. Phoibe Holmes, of Los Angeles, is over ninety years old, yet very beautiful in body and alert in mind. She says that her husband was so excellent in spirits and so good to her during his lifetime that their married life was like heaven on earth. His going, when she was between sixty and seventy, left her prostrate. She became very ill and was thought to be dying. Jesus appeared to her and healed her, and told her that her best work was still ahead; in fact, that her work had hardly begun. Since then she has written books, taught health classes, and given numerous lectures.

"A remarkable Methodist minister in Georgia, affectionately called 'The Bishop of the Wire Grass,' reports in his autobiography that when he was pastor at Sandersville, Georgia, and became very ill, everyone in the community prayed for his recovery. A little Catholic girl counted her beads. He says that for a while he saw both worlds at the same time; then he lost sight of this world and saw Jesus and those with Him on the other side. In the experience he appeared almost to be reaching the heavenly shore; his first wife and the children had grown up. Everyone who had heard him preach and who believed and had passed over was also there to welcome him. Just before he reached the other shore, Jesus said to him, 'I have more work for you to do on earth.' The 'Bishop of the Wire Grass' says that he did not want to come back, yet wanted to please Jesus.

"A Mrs. Kennedy, nee Gladys Perkins, appeared to have been away from her body about twenty minutes when she was living in Bellevue, a suburb of Macon. The friend with her continued to pray and life returned. Mrs. Kennedy reported that she had been in the presence of Jesus and had seen, but not been allowed to touch, her mother and others who were with Him."

Manifest Victory, Logos International, Plainfield, N.J. 07061. Used by permission.

He that hath my commandments, and keepeth them, he it is that loveth me: and he that loveth me shall be loved of my Father, and I will love him, and will manifest myself to him.

* * * * *

Roxanne Brant: Vision into Worship

Prior to her preparation for the ministry, Roxanne Brant studied to be a concert pianist and medical doctor. However, one day while studying in a library, she had a powerful confrontation with Christ which changed her from a militant agnostic into a Christian. She is presently minister-president of Outreach for Christ, Inc., traveling many miles each year. In addition to her studies at Gordon Divinity School, she has studied at Harvard Divinity School and Boston University School of Theology.

Several years ago, something very supernatural and unforgettable occurred that left a mark on me. It taught me that (1) my first ministry is to the Lord and (2) that to praise Him without worshiping Him is not enough. The Lord Himself came and showed me these things; He taught me the difference between praise and worship. It happened one evening while I was ministering in a charismatic Presbyterian church. The songleader had led the congregation for about twenty minutes in singing the usual songs of praise and thanksgiving to God for healing, prospering and saving people—songs such as, "Amazing Grace," "He Touched Me," "Blessed Assurance," and others.

When it was time to speak, the minister arose and began to introduce me. Suddenly, to the right of the minister I saw Jesus. He was standing there with the loneliest expression I have ever seen on any face. His soft brown eyes overflowed with tears which began to pour down His cheeks and drop silently at His feet. There was no noise, no sobbing, and no movement of anything but the tears as they silently streamed down His face and dropped to the floor. The sense of His loneliness filled my being and I wanted to comfort Him. How lonely He was, even in the midst of all His people.

He disappeared as suddenly as He had appeared, but I knew in an instant why He had been weeping. He was lonely because in spite of all our self-centered singing *about* Him, He Himself was completely ignored. No wonder He wept; of course He was lonely. My mind was so filled with what I had seen, that when I came to the realization that I had just been introduced to the congregation, I seemed unable to speak. I arose and turned to them, still choking down the sobs which filled me, but I managed to speak several words. All I could say was, ''Now, let's worship Jesus.''

Immediately it seemed as if the Holy Spirit flooded the sanctuary and began to move like a soft wind through a giant, divine harp. For the next fifteen to twenty minutes everyone in the congregation began singing in the spirit such exquisitely beautiful arrangements as no human mind could conceive. The Holy Spirit was using our bodies as instruments for the expression of His own worship to the Lord Jesus Christ. He had heard our feeble attempts to praise Jesus, but now He filled our vocal apparatus with His own perfect, holy songs of worship.

How indispensable we were to each other, the Spirit and each of us! I remember, particularly, how a man on one side of the auditorium and a woman on the other kept singing cascades of prophetic worship up and down the scale in perfect harmony as they worshiped the Lord in the Spirit. It sounded as if passages out of the book of Revelation were being brought to life. There was such a glorious, festal presence of the Holy Spirit that we felt as if we were in a heavenly banquet and that any minute we could put our hand on the arm of the King of Kings and march right up the aisle with Him. After some time, the Holy Spirit gradually lifted His hand from us and I knew it was time for the message. Again, Jesus spoke very clearly to me and said, "You have ministered to me, so now I will minister to you." Then I arose and gave a message on "Ministering To The Lord."

I share this with you because I am convinced that Jesus is all too frequently lonely at the services we claim to hold in His name. So many services are centered only in praise, which generally speaks of what God has done for us, but can ignore His presence with us. This is not enough, for we also need services which are centered in worship, a worship in which the believer is caught up in the present reality of God's person, in the reality of who He is.

Reverend Roxanne Brant, a graduate of Gordon Divinity School, conducts crusades and healing services throughout the United States and Canada. Excerpt taken from *Ministering to the Lord* published by Outreach for Christ, Inc., Naples, Florida, copyright © 1973.

O come, let us worship and bow down: let us kneel before the Lord our maker. For he is our God; and we are the people of his pasture, and the sheep of his hand. To-day if ye will hear his voice. . . .

Psalm 95:6,7

At that time the Lord separated the tribe of Levi, to bear the ark of the covenant of the Lord, to stand before the Lord to minister unto him, and to bless in his name, unto this day.

Deuteronomy 10:8

But the hour cometh, and now is, when the true worshipers shall worship the Father in spirit and in truth: for the Father seeketh such to worship him. God is a Spirit: and they that worship him must worship him in spirit and in truth.

John 4:23,24

What is it then? I will pray with the spirit, and I will pray with the understanding also: I will sing with the spirit, and I will sing with the understanding also.

1 Corinthians 14:15

Treena Kerr's
Vision of Jesus

Treena Kerr, actress and wife of Graham Kerr, TV's "Galloping Gourmet," tells of her beautiful conversion and vision of Jesus in a small Black church in Maryland.

On 17th of December 1974: Propelled by God's hand on my shoulder and led by my friend Ruth Turner, I found and saw sweet Jesus.

While the congregation was praying for me, a feeling of suffocation happened with a terrible undulation in my stomach, and a scream flew from me. I fell on my knees and wept; not tears, but waterfalls, flowed out of my eyes and I was saying "forgive me Jesus, forgive me Jesus, I'm sorry Jesus" and I felt so sad and full of remorse. No one noticed what had happened save my daughter; truly now, this was a deliverance, but of course I did not know it at the time.

When the congregation finally finished praying, I was baptised totally in water. Later I was asked if I'd like to tarry for the Holy Spirit. I said yes, as I was there I might as well. I asked Ruthie what I should do. She said "thank Jesus" so I knelt down and kept saying "thank you Jesus" not understanding at all what I should do. Finally, I was so hot and felt really ridiculous and thought my impending commitment into a mental home was a necessity. While thinking to myself—"this is crazy, what are you doing"—a great light fell on my face and I thought "Huh, now they have turned the church lights up to make me think I've got what I'm suppose to get" (the suspicion of the actress mind was very much to the fore) so I opened my eyes and there standing in front of me was this man, all in white, with the most beautiful smile, a smile of all the love in the world, just for me. He spoke and laid His hand on my heart. Praise Jesus! To my chagrin I can't remember exactly what He said and I don't want to put words down that aren't true; however, the gist of it was, "Wait, you have received, but it's not time yet."

I received the manifestation two months later in the kitchen all by myself, never having heard tongues spoken.

The church was, believe it or not, in a little place called Bethlehem, in Preston, Maryland, and it was an all black church. Tessa, my daughter, Michele, our secretary, and I were the only whites in that happy lovely black church. It was the first time I had been to church in eighteen years. I had never read the Bible until two days previously and I didn't believe in Jesus, but I certainly did afterwards! I praise the beloved Lord for choosing, wanting and saving me, for like Thomas I would never have believed had I not seen Him and been touched and consequently completely changed.

Then saith he to Thomas, Reach hither thy finger, and behold my hands; and reach hither thy hand, and thrust it into my side: and be not faithless, but believing. And Thomas answered and said unto him, My Lord and my God.

John 20:27,28

But God commendeth his love toward us, in that, while we were yet sinners, Christ died for us.

Romans 5:8

That Christ may dwell in your hearts by faith; and ye, being rooted and grounded in love, May be able to comprehend with all saints what is the breadth and length, and depth, and height.

Ephesians 3:17-19

* * * * *

Battlefield Experience

The following story is taken from "Life and Word," the Church of Scotland magazine:

I remember the very hour when George Casey turned to me with a queer look in his blue eyes and asked if I had seen the Friend of the Wounded.

And then he told me all he knew. After many a hot engagement, a man in white had been seen bending over the wounded. Snipers shot at him. Shells fell all around. Nothing had power to touch him. He was either heroic beyond all heroes, or he was something greater still. This mysterious one, whom the French called the "Comrade in White," seemed to be everywhere at once. At Nancy, in the Argonne, at Soissons and Ypres, everywhere men were talking of Him in hushed voices.

I, who was often reckless in my talk, said, "Seeing is believing."

The next day our big guns roared from sunrise to sunset, and began again in the morning. We had advanced one hundred fifty yards when we found it was no good. Our captain called to us to take cover, and just then I was shot through both legs.

By God's mercy I fell into a hole of some sort, I suppose I fainted, for when I opened my eyes I was all alone. The pain was horrible, but I didn't dare to move lest the Germans should see me, for they were only fifty yards away, and I did not expect mercy. I was glad when the twilight came. There were men in my own company who would run any risk in the darkness if they thought a comrade was still alive.

The night fell and soon I heard a step, not stealthy as I expected but quiet and firm, as if neither darkness, nor death could check those untroubled feet. So little did I guess what was coming that even when I saw the gleam of white in the darkness I thought it was a peasant in a white smock, or perhaps, a woman in white. Suddenly, with a little shiver of fear, I don't know which, I guessed that it was the "Comrade in White." And at that very moment the German rifles began to shoot.

The bullets could scarcely miss such a target, for he flung out his arms as though in entreaty. And he spoke. The words sounded familiar, but all I remember was the beginning: "If thou hadst known," and the ending, "but now they are hid

44

from thine eyes." And then he stopped and gathered me into his arms—me, the biggest man in the regiment—and carried me as if I had been a child.

I must have fainted again, for I awoke to consciousness in a little cave by a stream, and the Comrade in White was washing my wounds and binding them up. It seems foolish to say it, for I was in terrible pain, but I was happier at that moment than ever I remember to have been in all my life before. I can't explain it, but it seemed as if all my days I had been waiting for this without my knowing it. As long as that hand touched me and those eyes pitied me, I did not seem to care any more about sickness or health, about life, or death.

I could see, as it were, a shot wound in his hand, and as he prayed, a drop of blood gathered and fell to the ground. I cried out. I could not help it, for that wound of his seemed to me a more awful thing than any that bitter war had shown me.

"You are wounded, too," I said, faintly. Perhaps he heard me, perhaps it was the look on my face, but he answered gently: "This is an old wound, but it has troubled me of late." And then I noticed sorrowfully that the same cruel mark was on his feet. You will wonder that I did not know sooner. I wonder myself. But it was only when I saw His feet I knew Him.

"The Living Christ—I had heard the chaplain say it a few weeks before, but now I knew that He had come to me—to me who had put Him out of my life in the hot fever of my youth. I was longing to speak and thank Him, but no words came. And then He arose swiftly and said: "Lie here today by the water. I will come for you tomorrow. I have work for you to do and you will do it for me."

In a moment He was gone. And while I wait for Him my pain increases but I have His promise, He will come for me tomorrow.

From *Angels,* a tract written by James Check, published by Osterhus Publishing House, Minneapolis, Minnesota.

The Lord hath appeared of old unto me, saying, Yea, I have loved thee with an everlasting love: therefore with lovingkindness have I drawn thee.

Jeremiah 31:3

Yea, though I walk through the valley of the shadow of death, I will fear no evil: for thou art with me; thy rod and thy staff they comfort me.

Psalm 23:4

* * * * *

Michael Esses:
"Michael, Michael, Why Do You Hate Me?"

Michael Esses was an orthodox Jew and the son of a rabbi with the largest congregation of Judean Jews in New York. He was rebellious as a child, but is now a humble, Spirit-led Christian who is a popular Old Testament teacher and scholar at Melodyland School of the Bible in California. He makes extensive speaking engagements around the world.

The words she said hit me like a hammer. "Mike, I want a divorce. I have spent most of my life with your miserable disposition and your grudges. You've made my existence a living hell most of the time. I have endured it because I loved you and thought that you loved me in spite of how you treated me. I realize now that I've just been kidding myself. There is something very basic missing in you, and while I feel sorry for you, I won't subject myself or these children to you any longer.

"God knows, with Kathy,* my burden is hard enough, and Mike, I just can't carry you any longer. If you will take my advice, you will seek out God and let Him help you become a man who can look at himself in the mirror again. I will be praying for you, as I have done since the first day I met

---

Their ill daughter

46

you."

Then she heaped some burning coals on my head when she said, "I have to ask you to forgive me for the harsh words I said to you this morning. I really don't want anything for you except the best. If I hadn't been beside myself with anger, I would never have said what I did. Believe me, I want only the best for you."

When we went to bed that night, I lay there for quite a while contemplating what I had done. It reminded me of a small boy who has built a castle out of blocks and yet he can't resist the urge to turn around and kick the whole thing down. Why was I like this? What had happened to the rabbi who was raised to love God before anything else? Why did I find it impossible to forgive Him for the misfortunes in my life? This unforgiveness in my soul was not going to cost me my wife and children. Betty lay beside me, but she might as well have been a million miles away. I could have reached out and touched her, but I knew it would do no good, for she had withdrawn herself from me. I had no one. I was alone. The arrogant stubborn man was reduced to a lost child again.

I finally fell into a deep sleep, from which I was aroused some time later by a feeling that someone was in the room. I sat up in bed and looked over at Betty. She was fast asleep. The hands on the luminous dial on the bedside clock showed a few minutes after two. Then I looked to my left, and there, standing in a soft glow, was a figure with His hands outstretched toward me.

I could feel my heart begin to pound, as fright washed over me. Then the figure spoke my name.

"Michael, Michael."

I was too frightened to answer.

He spoke again. "Michael, Michael."

This time I swallowed and asked, "What do You want?"

With a soft voice that contained all the compassion of the ages, all the love that any man could ever require, and all the gentleness of a mother holding her first-born child, He said,

47

"Why do you hate Me?"

The frightened man, the arrogant man, was still in charge.

"Hate you? I don't even know who the heck You are."

The figure vanished. He was gone, and I was once again alone. Completely alone. I found myself in a cold sweat, trembling, and shaking. I also seemed to be unable to stop sobbing. I glanced over at Betty, and she was still in a sound sleep, so I slipped out of the bed and began to wander through the house. I went from room to room, trying to get away from the turmoil that filled every fiber of my being. Peace. My God, how I wanted to feel some measure of peace.

Hours went by, in which I felt like my very soul was being scourged. The faint light of dawn was beginning to filter through the drapes when I found myself in the den. I cast my eyes over the bookcase, looking for something to read, something to occupy my mind.

My eyes lit upon the little Hebrew New Testament that I had received so many years ago. My hand seemed drawn to it by a force I couldn't explain. I took it down from its perch on the highest shelf and began to leaf through it.

Then it seemed that an even deeper stillness began to fill the house. I could no longer hear the ticking of the clock. The everwhirring motor of the refrigerator ceased its steady sound, and a silent hush that filled me with expectancy came over the room.

The only sound that existed on this earth was the faint rustle of the pages of the Bible as they finally came to rest. They were open at the Gospel of John, and as I looked upon the pages, the 24th and 25th verses of the 20th chapter seemed to leap out at me:

"But Thomas, one of the twelve, called Didymus, was not with them when Jesus came.

The other disciples therefore said unto him, we have seen the Lord. But he said unto them, except I shall see in his hands the print of the nails, and put my finger into the print of the nails, and thrust my hand into his side, I will not believe.''

The knowledge, the realization, the recognition of Him who had stood by my bed and asked that agonizing question, ''Why do you hate Me?'' floated over me like a tidal wave.

The nail prints in his hands. Oh, my God! That glowing figure that stood at the side of my bed had had the nail prints in His hands. I remembered seeing them, and the mark upon His side.

The exaltation that filled my soul was too much to ever describe. I had not only found my God again, but my Messiah as well. I could feel the unhappiness, the bitterness, the arrogance begin to flow out of my body like a steady stream, while a surging river began to fill me with peace, hope, steadiness, and love. Yes, love. I was going through a baptism of love.

I fell to my knees and gave Christ my life. I was truly being born again. It was a new man who uttered the words of profession, ''You are my Messiah, and my God.''

From *Michael, Michael, Why Do You Hate Me?*, by Michael Esses, Logos International Plainfield, N.J. 07061, copyright © 1973.

For I am not ashamed of the gospel of Christ: for it is the power of God unto salvation to every one that believeth; to the Jew first, and also to the Greek.

Romans 1:16

And many other signs truly did Jesus in the presence of his disciples, which are not written in this book: But these are written, that ye might believe that Jesus is the Christ, the Son of God; and that believing ye might have life through his name.

John 20:30,31

* * * * *

Startling Incidents
This article appeared in the British National Sunday newspaper, The People, *which has a two million circulation*

Dr. Kenneth Symonds, surgeon and physician, sat in his room at the Swansea Hospital where he is the senior medical officer and said: "I must affirm that the recovery of Melita Floyd is nothing less than a miracle—perhaps the greatest miracle of modern times. It has nothing whatever to do with bottles of medicine and the skill of doctors."

That is, indeed, the only possible way of explaining what has happened to 35-year-old Miss Floyd.

For thirty years she was a total cripple, tied to a bed and unable even to sit up or even move her legs. Doctors pronounced her case as hopeless.

Today, with the aid of sticks, she can walk. From her home with her married sister in Park Street, Neath, she goes shopping.

She can type. She is learning to play the piano. She is the girl who came back from the grave. And her cure, according to Dr. Symonds, is entirely due to another woman and to the faith both she and Melita have in the healing powers of God.

It is three years ago since Mrs. Elsie Salmon, the wife of a Methodist minister, laid hands on Melita Floyd at a healing service in Treherbert Methodist Church.

At once the miracle happened. But no one has dared to talk about it in case Miss Floyd suffered a relapse.

But now there is no doubt about it. She is permanently cured. In the first three months after the service she grew *seventeen inches*.

Dr. Symonds is best able to describe Miss Floyd's condition, for as senior medical officer of the Bible College Hospital at Swansea, he has had a close knowledge of her case for sixteen years.

On the day of the service she was completely paralysed as the result of tuberculosis of the spine. She weighed a mere 35 pounds.

Her legs were no thicker than a man's thumb and they were

permanently bent under her.

"I have never seen such an advanced case of this kind," Dr. Symonds told me. "Physically, Miss Floyd was a complete wreck. She was beyond all hope."

Her condition was made worse by her mental condition, for her mother, who was her constant nurse and companion, had just died. Grief at the separation was intense for the daughter.

In Miss Floyd's own words: "On the night of the service I just wanted to die and be with my mother."

But friends insisted on carrying her to the church for the healing service.

Melita Floyd describes what happened in these words:

"Mrs. Salmon placed her hands on me. She began to pray. Suddenly I felt something very cold, like ice. A white mist seemed to come up in front of me.

"It was a wonderful white, and then suddenly it broke. And out of the mist came the Saviour Himself—just His head and His hands.

"I was lost and I said: 'Oh, Lord Jesus, You have got my mother and I no longer mind . . . just to spend eternity with You.' "

Then Melita found herself back in the church, with Mrs. Salmon, who kissed her and said: "You will walk, my dear."

Only then did the miracle begin.

Two days later Melita was at home in her bed when there was a sharp cracking noise.

"What's that?" called her sister.

"It's coming from inside me," said Melita.

And it was so. Every day for the next three months the cracking noises could be heard all over her room, and her legs began to move.

Rapidly, her weight increased and soon Melita found she could sit up without support.

Then came the day when she left her bed and dressed.

So it went on, month after month, a recovery so astonishing that Dr. Symonds could scarcely believe it.

"It is a miracle that to me is unshakeable proof that the words of the Lord know no bounds," he told me.

From an article in *The Evidence* by Peter Forbes, Vol. 20, No. 1, an Interdenominational Quarterly.

Now there is at Jerusalem by the sheep market a pool, which is called in the Hebrew tongue Bethesda, having five porches. In these lay a great multitude of impotent folk, of blind, halt, withered, waiting for the moving of the water. For an angel went down at a certain season into the pool, and troubled the water: whosoever then first after the troubling of the water stepped in was made whole of whatsoever disease he had. And a certain man was there, which had an infirmity thirty and eight years. When Jesus saw him lie, and knew that he had been now a long time in that case, he saith unto him, Wilt thou be made whole? The impotent man answered him, Sir, I have no man, when the water is troubled, to put me into the pool: but while I am coming, another steppeth down before me. Jesus saith unto him, Rise, take up thy bed, and walk. And immediately the man was made whole, and took up his bed, and walked: and on the same day was the sabbath.

John 5:2-9

* * * * *

Blind Woman Sees Again

The story of Mrs. Mary Boese is told in the May 11, 1965 issue of Chicago American (Chicago Today). She had been blind for two years.

Mrs. Boese is a religious woman. She knew she would see again—even when doctors said she never would. Mrs. Boese said she had seen a vision of Christ and felt this was a sign her vision would be returned.

"He smiled at Me."

"I knew because of the way He smiled at me that I would see again." She said she had the vision immediately after being examined by eye doctors in Oklahoma City. Three doctors had just told her she would never see again.

"I was totally blind at the time," she said. "My daughter was leading me down the hall. I saw this light coming towards me. It was a different kind. It glowed, and all at once there was Jesus standing there. He held His hands up in front of Him. He didn't say anything to me. I knew He didn't want me to come yet. I was ready."

. . . She happily recounted the moment her sight returned.

"I had gone into the bathroom about 5:40 A.M. I suddenly started seeing things—toothpaste, a comb, towels around. There were so many things. I felt that I had my glasses on and that my glasses certainly must have improved. I felt, and I didn't have any glasses on.

"I combed my hair for 30 minutes," she said. "It sounds vain, but two years is a long time not to see your hair."

Used by permission, *Chicago American* (*Chicago Today*) Newspaper 441 N. Michigan Ave., Chicago, Illinois, Vol. 65 No. 264.

The Spirit of the Lord is upon me, because he hath anointed me to preach the gospel to the poor; he hath sent me to heal the brokenhearted, to preach deliverance to the captives, and recovering of the sight to the blind, to set at liberty them that are bruised, to preach the acceptable year of the Lord.   *Luke 4:18, 19*

* * * * *

A Voice From the Military
The C.L. Wilgus Story
As a young naval officer, several years ago, I found the joy and thrill of the new birth. I had heard the story of Jesus many times, and I thought I was a Christian. However, one Sunday

morning in a little country church I heard it anew, and God opened my spiritual eyes and unstopped my spiritual ears. I was not seeking Jesus that Sunday morning; but someone had been praying, and He was seeking me.

At the close of the service an invitation was given for sinners to give their lives to Christ. I looked around at the congregation and told myself I was as good as anyone there and no one had better invite me to go forward. I made up my mind if that happened, I was going out the back door. When no person could help me to find salvation, the Holy Spirit gave the personal invitation! The presence of the Lord was there with such power that I began to tremble. He gave me a choice: ''Christ, or a cocktail glass. You choose this day!'' I couldn't resist His invitation to accept Christ as my Saviour, so I went forward and fell on my knees at the altar, overwhelmed at His concern for and knowledge of me. That moment a peace came into my heart that has continually flooded my soul ever since, even in times of danger and trial—and there have been several such times.

One of the great experiences of my life as a Christian occurred several years ago while flying a four-engine aircraft from an airfield in Florida. I was an Ensign Plane Commander at the time and pilot of the aircraft. I had completely given my life to the Lord a few months earlier.

We had just taken off from the airfield when number two engine blew the exhaust stack loose, allowing flames to enter the nacelle area where fuel, oil lines and oil tanks were located. We quickly reduced power on that engine and continued climbing on the three good ones. The aircraft was quite heavy and we were still very low, so we did not stop the engine completely by ''feathering'' the propeller into the wind. Instead, we closed the throttle and set full low rpm to obtain minimum drag.

We climbed a few hundred feet, then turned back toward the airfield. The other three engines were getting hot. Suddenly number one engine ''seized'' internally and was completely stopped. The propeller, however, was turning so fast all the nose section bolts sheared. Oil ran back on the red-hot exhaust stacks and the whole engine was on fire. I ordered, "Feather number one," and reached for the throttles to get maximum power. The plane was dropping so fast I realized we couldn't clear the trees immediately below. To myself I said, "So this is how I'm going to die!" There wasn't a doubt in my mind but that I had just travelled my last mile.

At that instant I had a vision—Jesus was standing with arms outstretched waiting for me. I remembered my name was written in the Lamb's Book of Life—that I was a child of God. A feeling of peace, joy and sheer ecstasy swept over me. I saw another figure standing there—but sideways to me. I recognized him immediately as "Death," but his hands, which were behind his back, were bound together. Death could not touch me and the Lord was waiting for me with open arms! I cried out, "Jesus, save us!" That huge airplane sailed over the tree tops and did not crash. I don't know how—only it was the Lord.

We were now so low I planned to ditch the plane in the ocean near shore, but unaccountably it continued to hold some altitude and airspeed. We were just clearing the wave tops when I saw an unused runway that was too short for the big planes, and was closed to all aircraft. We turned quickly, landed safely, and were able to stop at the very end of the runway.

Our God is able to do anything!

From *Voice* Magazine, July-Aug. 1970, by Cmdr. Carl L. Wilgus, United States Navy. Used with permission of Dr. Raymond W. Becker, editor.

I sought the Lord, and he heard me, and delivered me from all my fears. They looked unto him, and were lightened: and their faces were not ashamed. This poor man cried, and the Lord heard him, and saved him out of his troubles.

Psalm 34:4-6

The Healing Christ

Genevieve Parkhurst, a clergyman's wife whose home is in Woodward, Oklahoma, had been told by her physician that she had a large lump in her right breast. Before she had set a date for surgery, Mrs. Parkhurst experienced the following:

One afternoon I stretched out on a bed, leaned against a pile of pillows, and opened a new book. It was *You Are My Friends* by Frank Laubach. I do not remember what I read; it was something about the friendship of Jesus, but the pictures in the back of the book fascinated me. Here were the great artists' conceptions of Jesus. There was "Christ Blessing the Children," by Plockhorst; "The Hope of the World," Copping; "Follow Me," the picture of the smiling Christ, by Curry; "Christ at Thirty," by Hoffman; "The Son of Man," by Sallman. . . . With each, I grasped a fuller revelation of Jesus. He became so real that I was lost in His holiness and His love. I loved Him as I had never loved Him before, for I knew Him as I had not known Him before.

When I came to the picture of "Christ in the Garden," by Hoffman, the very heart went out of me. Jesus knew what I was facing. Oh, how He knew! He had faced death and said, "Not my will, but thine be done." He said, "No man taketh my life from me. I lay it down of myself." He had walked steadily to His cross. But He had died to redeem a world, while I was just going to die. Oh! That there might be some good come from my dying!

"Oh, Christ, glorify Thyself through me," I prayed, pouring out my heart to Him.

Suddenly my breath stopped. I stared, spellbound, for there before me was the physical presence of Jesus. He was standing in a profile, His face lifted, as the face in Hoffman's painting. I held my breath as that radiant face turned, slowly, and His eyes looked straight into mine.

Oh! The eyes of Jesus! Nothing in this world can ever be as wonderful as His eyes. They held the wisdom of infinity, they were so understanding, so compassionate, so full of love. Those eyes held mine. They drank me, as the sun drinks the dew. I felt absorbed by His love. The room was full of light, and that light was His Presence.

Illusion? Some might call it that. But what followed was no illusion. As I felt the oneness of being absorbed by Christ, there was a sharp stab of pain in my right breast. The fingers of pain ran down my side to my waist and out my arm to the elbow. My hand flew to my breast. My attention had turned to myself, and when I again looked up, the Presence was gone.

But the lump was gone too! Completely gone! I laid three fingers in the hole where the lump had been, pushing the loose skin into the emptiness.

Gone! There was no soreness, only an empty place. I took off my blouse and in amazement looked at the loose flesh that was left. I sat down trembling.

Why had such a thing happened to me? I was not worthy of such a blessing. I had not even prayed that He would heal me. It had not occurred to me. I believed the Christian life was to give one strength to live, and fortitude to die. This was an outpouring of pure grace; the evidence of divine favor, unasked and unmerited.

I walked out, and once more sought the mountain top. But I walked on into life of His giving, from Gethsemane into Pentecost. So wonderful was the miracle that I could not speak of it. Jesus must have had a reason for telling those whom He healed, to tell no man.

As the days passed, the tissues filled in according to the normal process of body building. It took eight months for the process to be complete. Then it was perfect, and has been during the years which have passed.

From *The Healing Christ and Lessons from My School of Prayer*, Genevieve Parkhurst, 1964, Macalester Park Publishing Co., Minneapolis, Minn.

Bless the Lord, O my soul: and all that is within me, bless his holy name. Bless the Lord, O my soul, and forget not all his benefits: Who forgiveth all thine iniquities; who healeth all thy diseases; Who redeemeth thy life from destruction; who crowneth thee with lovingkindness and tender mercies.

Psalm 103:1-4

*   *   *   *   *

Jake Saw the Man with Holes in His Hands!

I was lost in a snowstorm one night high up in the Smoky Mountains of Tennessee. Though I was frozen into unconsciousness, my horse carried me to a house. When consciousness began to dawn again, I heard a fire crackling at my feet, and, looking up, saw a bearded man bending over, swearing because I would not open my mouth to admit the neck of a bottle. In that moment of delirium, I thought I was dead and had gone to the wrong place.

When my senses returned, I recognized the man as a notorious outlaw with a price on his head, a man who had vowed that physical violence would fall heavily on any preacher who dared to enter his house, and I did not know what to expect.

No man could have treated me more kindly; for my rescuer and his wife did everything possible for me. When bedtime came, he took me in bed with him and held me against his great warm breast all night, never relaxing his vigilance for a moment. In the morning I was little worse for my experience, but the sun shone and the snow was melting, and I was ready to go. Then it was that something said, "You have a chance that no other preacher ever had and you must try to save Jake Woods."

How should I begin? Jake was sitting before the wide fireplace as I packed my saddlebags. I walked over to him. Taking a bill from my pocket, I said, "Mr. Woods, I regret to offer you so little, when you and your good wife have done so much for me, but this is a little expression of my appreciation for what you have done. I could not repay you, even if I were rich."

He looked me over from head to foot with astonishment.

"Put up your money, Doc," he said. "What we done for you was because we wanted to be clever to you. If you had come to my house last night as a preacher, I would have turned you away in the storm and been glad if you were frozen to death this morning. Twenty odd years ago when the Almighty took my boy, our only child, I swore that no man representing Him should ever come under my roof, and I kept my word until last night; but when your horse brought you I couldn't turn you away. Now you can go and say that you have stayed all night with Jake Woods."

His last sentence was hissed through clenched teeth. I never saw a man look so fierce. Certainly I had done all I could and failed, so I picked up my saddlebags from the bedside and started toward the door. But something gripped my conscience with fingers like steel. "You must try again," the unmistakable order came.

I walked the floor time and again to find a ship to Tarshish, but none was in sight. I was sure that he guessed what I was suffering, but he never turned his head. Finally, I walked over to him again, and with a voice trembling from emotion, I said, "Mr. Woods, I have a little book that I want to read and talk to a Friend of mine before I go; will you let me?" He turned to his wife, sitting in the corner, and said, "Doc, it's all right; go ahead." I began reading that wonderful chapter of Luke, about that one sheep that strayed, but was found.

There was the story of the prodigal son, too. When he came home in tatters within and without, his father was so happy that he would gladly have killed everything on the place to make merry because his son had come.

Just then I looked out of the corner of my eye and Jake Woods had turned around and was looking at me with eager interest, as much as to say, "What are you talking about me for?" I was, for he had sneered in the messenger's face who came when his father was dying and begged his son to come home.

I dropped to my knees and took hold of God with one hand and tried to reach Jake Woods with the other, but he was too far down. I held on and reached for Woods until I remembered that the sin of lacking hospitality is unpardonable with us. I said, "O God, I came here more dead than alive last night, and this man and his good wife took me in and nursed me back to life, and now they refused to accept anything for their kindness. But Jesus Christ has stood at their door ever since they have had a house with outstretched hands bleeding and with thorn-crowned brow, and they have slammed the door in His face. Help Jake Woods to tell Jesus Christ to come in today."

When I got up, Woods was sitting on the floor, looking at the door. I followed his gaze but saw nothing but the open door, with the sunshine and melting snow. After a minute, he said to something apparently in the door, "Come in." Then turning to me, he added, "He came in," as much as to say, "You can't throw it up to me anymore."

When I left the cabin, he followed me to the gate. "Doc," he asked, "have you another of those little books like you read out of a while ago? My pap used to read about that boy, and I guess I've been him. If you'll lend me one and turn down a leaf, I might find someone to read, and I think I would like to hear it again."

I gave him the Book and he turned away, saying that his "old woman" might come to hear me preach when I returned to the Flats schoolhouse again.

Several times before I had preached at the Flats, sometimes to a few good souls, but when I arrived this time, the whole campus seemed to be covered with people. The first man who met me and gripped my hand until I thought I would fall off my horse, was Jake Woods. "Doc, I fetched 'em," was his greeting, and he had.

I walked into the schoolhouse. The women were on one side of the aisle. On the end of the second bench from the front there was one who caught my coat sleeve as I passed. I looked down into her upturned face. It was Nancy Woods, at church for the first time in more than twenty years.

"Doc," she said, "there is something the matter with Jake."

"What like?" I asked.

"I don't know, but he ain't like he used to be since you were there. He's been really good to me. Doc, please call for mourners today; maybe Jake'll go up."

The tears came to my eyes as I walked on to the table and laid my saddlebags down.

Jake Woods had beaten that woman almost to death once because she had given a coin to a preacher. Many times he had driven her off in the storm to perish. Once, in a drunken delirium, he had thrown her into the fire. Now she had been in heaven for three whole weeks.

I turned, and there the men came, with Jake Woods at their head, walking like he was on air. Just behind him was an old soldier of the Civil War, hopping on a stiff knee. He hadn't been in church since the war closed. Woods sat at the end of the front bench, and the old soldier by his side. I shall never forget how the old man dropped down and adjusted his stiff leg, then crossed his hands with eager resignation, as he looked up in my face, as much as to say, "Well, I'm here."

The house was full of good and bad. The sermon that I had prepared would not fit, so I took for my text, "The Son of Man is come to seek and to save that which was lost."

I don't think I ever so preached before or since, but somebody standing by that table did preach that day with power and conviction.

61

When I was ready to let down the net, Jake Woods sprang to his feet and went down the aisle, speaking in a voice that drowned mine: "Men and women, come on! Doc's telling you the truth; for I saw that Man when Doc prayed in my house. When I opened my eyes He was standing in the door with His hands stretched out, and there were holes in them with blood running out. I saw thorns on His head too. And I told him to come in and He came, and I haven't been the same man since."

They came until it seemed they all would come.

Jake Woods went out to exhort and save the people of his acquaintance, and he reached more of that class in the two years that he lived, than I could have reached in a lifetime.

Used by permission. Pilgrim Tract Society, Randleman, North Carolina 27317; Reverend J. S. Barnett, author.

I exhort therefore, that, first of all, supplications, prayers, intercessions, and giving of thanks, be made for all men; For kings, and for all that are in authority; that we may lead a quiet and peaceable life in all godliness and honesty. For this is good and acceptable in the sight of God our Saviour; Who will have all men to be saved, and to come unto the knowledge of the truth.

1 Timothy 2:1-4

* * * * *

My Personal Testimony

Dr. Ray Charles Jarman was ordained June 15, 1913, to the ministry in the Christian Church of the Disciples of Christ. Dr. Jarman preached for fifty-two years without knowing Jesus as his personal Saviour, nor even imagining what the ''born-again'' experience was. He pastored churches with memberships of more than a thousand, but did not have a single convert that he knew of. Then at the age of seventy, he was led to the reality of Jesus as a person and as a Savior. Dr. Jarman has tried many of the mental science

groups, including Religious Science, Yoga, Theosophy,
Christian Unity, all of the new thought groups, and was for
eighteen years a teacher of metaphysics over prominent
radio stations in Los Angeles before his conversion.

For fifty-two years I preached, not believing in the Bible
account of the birth of Jesus. I looked upon Jesus as the
greatest teacher. No one who had ever been born equaled
Him. Just as Abraham Lincoln was the greatest American
statesman, so Jesus was the greatest religious figure. He
excelled in mind, spiritual understanding, and in knowledge
of God. His words, therefore, were strong support to my
belief in God as Father and in the immortality of the soul. But
I did not believe in the Virgin Birth. . . .

Then one night Shannon called me [Shannon Vandruff, a
former member of Mr. Jarman's congregation] and said,
"Ray, I want to come to your apartment. I don't want to go
out to dinner. I just want to talk to you alone."

I answered, "All right, Shannon, come on." Somehow I
sensed that this was going to be a fateful night for me. It was
March 28, 1966. . . .

He approached me in a different way than any time before.
He immediately said, "Ray, you have been trying to find
Jesus the wrong way. You have been trying through wisdom,
reason, logic, theology, and rationalization to find Him, and
you'll never find Him that way. The Bible plainly tells you
that you won't. Jesus said, 'Unless you turn and become as a
little child, you shall in no wise enter the Kingdom of God! I
thank Thee, O Father, Lord of heaven and earth, that Thou
didst hide these things from the wise and understanding and
didst reveal them unto babes, for so it was well pleasing in
Thy sight.' "

He continued, "Ray, when a child comes to his mother, he
doesn't say, 'Prove that you love me. Convince me that you
can take care of me. Make me believe that you will answer
my every cry night and day.' No, he simply accepts the

63

loving arms of his mother. So it is with Jesus. Don't ask Him anything; don't question Him; just accept Him.''

Then I said something I had not planned on saying. But what I said proved to be the most important words that ever passed over my lips. I said, ''Shannon, I want Him.''

Suddenly I found myself on my knees. In all my years of preaching I had never prayed on my knees. I didn't think the position of the body was important. I thought that the people who prayed on their knees were foolish. But there I was on my knees sobbing. I cried so hard that Shannon began to be concerned about me and what might happen to me physically until he remembered that the Lord Jesus would take care of that. I seemed to be at the bottom of a black pit of tar, writhing around down there. A whole avalanche of doubts, fears, sins and past preaching broke loose from a mountain range that enveloped me and came pounding down upon me. The load of my sins was too great. God would never forgive me. Great drops of perspiration covered my brow as I turned my tear-soaked face up to Shannon and said, ''I give up. I can't do it, Shannon. I am too far away. God doesn't want me.''

And suddenly, and I mean suddenly, the greatest peace surrounded me! It seemed to be a plateau of peace that stretched out in front of me. I have never felt such peace before or since. I didn't know that such a state of rich peace existed. I was so relaxed and all of the burden of sin was taken away. It was beautiful and sweet.

Then I seemed to be in a large room with small square panels on all sides. The door in the back of it swung noiselessly open, and *Jesus* walked in. He came so smoothly right up to me and didn't say a word; the Divine lips were fast closed. He put His hands on my shoulders—His fingers were so long—and He saturated me with His love. I knew then I was born again in Christ Jesus.

I got up from my knees and said, ''Shannon, I want to read the Bible.''

He said, "Ray, just let it fall open wherever it will. Put your finger on one line and then read what is under your finger."

It fell open to the ninth chapter of Matthew, the second verse, and the last line which reads, "Be of good cheer, my son, your sins are forgiven." Praise God! It was God's message to me that night. God had spoken, and I believed.

About six weeks after this, Rev. Ralph Wilkerson spent a day with me in my office, and before the day was over I received the baptism in the Holy Spirit, speaking in a heavenly language. This second great blessing has given me the power to be an effective witness for the Lord. How grateful I am for it.

I had no idea what changes this would bring about in my life. Everything was different. I was a new creature socially, religiously, morally, and philosophically. Nothing was the same. I thought of the Bible in an entirely new way. My whole system of theology changed from that of a modernist and liberal to that of a conservative Bible believer. I now believe the Bible from cover to cover. I did not believe in the Virgin Birth, but now I *know* that Jesus was the Son of God and was born as the Bible tells us. That is the only way His blood could mean anything to me and the only way He could be my Saviour. I believe in the miracles, the resurrection, the ascension, and the Second Coming of our Lord. Indeed I can hardly wait for that glorious day!

As stated in a booklet written and printed by the Reverend Ray Charles Jarman, D.D. Used with permission.

Him that cometh to me I will in no wise cast out.

John 6:37b

All scripture is given by inspiration of God, and is profitable for doctrine, for reproof, for correction, for instruction in righteousness: That the man of God may be perfect, throughly furnished unto all good works.

2 Timothy 3:16-17

Then said Jesus to those Jews which believed on him, If ye continue in my word, then are ye my disciples indeed; And ye shall know the truth, and the truth shall make you free.

John 8:31-32

* * * * *

The Keys to Life

Dr. F.B. Meyer (1847-1929) of Christ Church, London, was a well-known Baptist clergyman at the turn of the century. He introduced Dwight L. Moody to the British churches, and from that time on was a life-long friend of the American evangelist. Meyer's ministry focused on social, temperance, and reclamation work, which led him into the political world. In addition, he was an author of several books which continue in their popularity today.

Dr. F.B. Meyer of Christ Church, London, was seated one day in his study engaged in deep meditation. He was disturbed over the fact that his ministry seemed to be unfruitful and lacking in spiritual power. He was cast into deep spiritual concern and distress. Suddenly Christ seemed to enter the room and stand beside him. "Let me have the key to your life," Christ said to him. The experience was so vivid that Meyer reached into his pocket to take out a bunch of keys. "Are all the keys of your life here?" asked Jesus as he slowly examined the keys placed in his hands. "Yes, Lord," said Meyer, "all the keys." Then with a sudden pang of conscience he added, "All the keys to the rooms in my life except one small room." At that time Meyer said that there was still one place in his life where he was not willing to give Christ full and final control.

The Lord slowly handed the keys back to Meyer saying sadly, "If you cannot trust me with all the keys to all the rooms in your life, I cannot accept any of the keys." Christ turned and started to walk out of the room. Meyer said that in

66

sudden alarm it came to him that Christ was somehow moving out of his life because he was shutting Him out from one of his interests in life. Meyer stood up and pleaded, "Come back to me, Lord, come back to me and I will give you all the keys of my life. You can have this last key, too." Christ took all the keys of all the rooms of Meyer's life in His hand, smiled upon him and then vanished.

Dr. Meyer said that from that time forward blessed communion with Christ continually flowed through his life and sources of power and blessings were opened up that he had never dreamed of before.

From *Let There Be Light* by Dr. Benjamin T. Browne, published by Fleming H. Revell Company, Old Tappan, New Jersey 07675. Copyright © 1956. Used with permission.

Commit thy way unto the Lord; trust also in him, and he shall bring it to pass.

Psalm 37:5

But seek ye first the kingdom of God, and his righteousness; and all these things shall be added unto you.

Matthew 6:33

* * * * *

Use Me!

Chaplain Carothers's remarkable career took him from a criminal youth to the position of chaplain in the U.S. Army. His belief and practice of thanking God in all situations is an inspiration to all.

I had received the Baptism in the Holy Spirit only a couple of months ago, yet it seemed I'd already lived a lifetime in this new dimension.

Now I was in for an encounter with the enemy in force. I was suddenly the victim of an unusual affliction. All my life I'd been strong as a horse and in top physical condition. Now every time I exerted myself in the least, my heart began to beat rapidly. I was weak and ached all over. Reluctantly I went to bed for a week. My condition didn't improve at all. I went to the hospital to see what the medical verdict would be, and they immediately slapped me on a stretcher and hustled me off to bed. Test after test gave no clue to what ailed me. I felt wretched, weak, and in pain, and it seemed to get worse instead of better. At this rate I'd just as soon be dead; all my energies seemed depleted, and the outlook was indeed bleak.

Then suddenly one night when I wondered if the end might be near, there was the strong impression: "Do you still trust Me?"

"Yes, Lord." I whispered it into the darkened room.

A quiet peace began to move through me, and I fell into a deep sleep.

The next morning I felt much better. The doctors insisted I stay in bed for a while, and I was grateful for days of prayer, praise, and study.

One day I was reading one of Glenn Clark's books, and I suddenly felt the voice within me ask: "Will you now live like Jesus?"

I could only answer: "Yes, Lord."

"But what about your thoughts and desires, are they pure?"

"No, Lord."

"Do you want them to be?"

"Oh, yes Lord. All my life I've struggled to overcome impure thoughts and desires."

"Will you give me all your impure thoughts?"

"Yes, Lord."

"Forever?"

"O yes, Lord. Forever."

Suddenly it was as if a heaviness had been lifted from me, as if a mist had parted and everything looked clean and pure. The door to the ward opened and a young nurse walked through. I followed her with my eyes. She was a beautiful young nurse, and all I could think was: "What a beautiful child of God!" There was not even a fleeting thought of temptation!

Back home from the hospital, I went to our prayer group and felt a strong impression to ask them to pray for me. I had always been the one to pray for others. Now I sat in the chair in the center of the group and they prepared to pray for me.

"What do you want us to ask God to do?"

I thought for a moment. "Ask God to use me more than ever," I said. They began to pray, and I suddenly saw in the Spirit, Jesus kneeling before me. He was holding my feet and rested His head on my knees. He said: "I don't want to use you. I want you to use Me!"

It was as if a door had opened into a new understanding of Jesus. He wants to give Himself for us each moment of our lives just as completely as He gave Himself on the cross. We have nothing to give Him; we have only to receive of Him."

From *Prison to Praise* by Merlin R. Carothers, published by Logos International, Plainfield, N.J. 07061, copyright © 1970. Used with permission.

Thou wilt keep him in perfect peace, whose mind is stayed on thee: because he trusteth in thee. Trust ye in the Lord for ever: for in the LORD JEHOVAH is everlasting strength.

Isaiah 26:3-4

* * * * *

I Have Come to Answer
Your Prayer

Kenneth Hagin is the founding president of the Kenneth E. Hagin Evangelistic Association, Inc. He has served in the ministry for forty years, and has authored many successful books on prayer, healing, faith, prophecy, and demonology. He is a well-known speaker for seminars and conferences throughout the world.

My wife and I had just returned to our home in Garland, Texas, after spending fifteen months in meetings in the state of California. We then held a meeting for our home church, the First Assembly of God in Garland. It was during the third week of this meeting that I had another supernatural visitation from the Lord.

At the close of my message one night a spirit of prayer descended upon the congregation and we all gathered around the altar to pray. We prayed for quite some time with a real burden of intercession and prayer.

After a while I got off my knees and sat down on the steps leading from the platform. I was sitting there with my eyes open, singing in other tongues as the spirit gave utterance, when suddenly I saw Jesus standing about three feet in front of me. He said, "I have come to answer your prayer."

I knew exactly what He was talking about, as I had been praying for sometime for my wife, before leaving California, as she had a goiter. It was growing larger and larger until now she was having choking spells. One night while we were sleeping in our house trailer in California I was awakened. I saw my wife as she was just about to go out the door. I rose up and took hold of her. Immediately I saw that she didn't know what she was doing. I got her to lie back down. She later said that she didn't realize actually what had happened. When she fell back asleep, I lay there praying.

From the time that we were first married I had sensed in my spirit that she would die at an early age, and I thought perhaps that this time was approaching. I prayed the rest of the night about this and said to the Lord, "I have obeyed You and have done Your will. I left my church and my family, and have been in the evangelistic field for many years. My wife stayed at home and was faithful to raise our children. I am still a young man (at that time I was in my thirties), and we have been married for many years. Please let me keep my wife."

In the vision the Lord said to me, "I have come to answer

70

that prayer. Tell your wife to be operated on, for she will live and not die.''

Although I didn't mention it to my wife, I had felt all along that if she were operated on she would die. She later told me that she had known for several years that she would die when she was operated on for this goiter.

But the Lord said to me, ''She will live and not die. It was divine destiny that she would die, but I have heard your prayers and have come to answer them. She shall live.''

Then Jesus said something that absolutely melted me and I have never been able to forget it. It blessed and helped me then and it still blesses me. He said, ''I did this, son, just because you asked me to. You don't know how I long to do for my children if they would only ask Me and believe Me. Many times they beg and cry and pray, but they don't believe. And I cannot answer their prayers unless they have faith, because I cannot violate my Word. But how often I long to help them if only they would let Me by taking Me at my Word and bringing Me their problems, trusting Me to undertake for them.'' Again He said, ''Tell your wife to be operated on, for she will live and not die.'' With those words He disappeared.

And even though the doctors were greatly concerned about my wife's condition, she and I had great joy through it all because we knew the outcome in advance.

From *I Believe in Visions* by Kenneth Hagin, published by Fleming H. Revell Company, Old Tappan, N. J., copyright © 1972. Used with permission.

Confess your faults one to another, and pray one for another, that ye may be healed. The effectual fervent prayer of a righteous man availeth much.

James 5:16

Jesus answered and said unto them, Verily I say unto you, if ye have faith, and doubt not, ye shall not only do this which is done to the fig tree, but also if ye shall say unto this mountain,

Be thou removed, and be thou cast into the sea: it shall be done. And all things, whatsoever ye shall ask in prayer, believing, ye shall receive.

Matthew 21:21-22

* * * * *

The Miracle Picture

The late Warner Sallman, a Chicago artist, painted nearly two dozen oil paintings of scenes in Christ's life. None is so famous as the "Head of Christ." He is also known for his chalk drawings of the head of Christ and wall-sized murals of Bible scenes.

Worried about an early morning deadline, Warner Sallman slept fitfully. Then he dreamed—a dream that taking form, shape and color became world renowned.

Sallman's paintings of Christ decorate igloos of Eskimos and huts of the Hottentots. They can be found in cathedrals of different faiths in many lands. Sallman's mail often brings to him testimonies from India, Africa, South America, Scandinavian countries, Canada, Australia and many other lands.

The story of this picture as well as of the artist himself is a miraculous one.

Back in 1917 a young commercial artist and a physician faced one another in the latter's office.

"The diagnosis is tuberculosis of the lymph glands. Surgery is your only hope," said the doctor. "Without surgery I believe you have about three months to live."

The artist left the office in a daze. His thought was not on himself but on the young singer who had only a few months before come his bride—and of their first baby they had just learned would be born.

Fortunately, Warner Sallman's wife was a Christian. "We will seek God's will," she said, "and we will thank

72

Him for the three months. We will ask Him to use us to the limit and if He mercifully gives us more, we shall be grateful for it.'' Together and in complete calmness of spirit they went to their God in prayer.

Without surgery, God performed a miracle of healing. Today, past 70, Sallman's rugged figure and robust enthusiasm are often seen in churches where he delights to do chalk illustrations of the head of Christ. His ministry in addition to the nearly two dozen oil paintings of various scenes in the life of Christ and the famous Head of Christ present a demonstration of God's grace in the life and ministry of Sallman.

Equally miraculous as this healing by the Lord is Sallman's experience in conceiving and drawing the Head of Christ for which he is famous the world over.

From time to time he aided his church publishing house by preparing art work for Sunday school papers. One day he was given an assignment to prepare a cover for one of these publications. Several times he had attempted to come up with an idea as he sat before his drawing board but nothing quite jelled as the deadline drew closer.

Now the thought flashed through his mind that he might make a sketch of Jesus for the cover illustration as the manly, cheerful, hope-inspiring Son of God and at the same time, the humble loving Savior.

By now, however, only 24 hours remained before the drawing was due. Up in his attic studio that evening, he went to work and completed the first sketch. But it wasn't what he wanted. He did another and another. More followed as Sallman's nerves grew taut, his mind feverish.

He agonized in prayer but with no immediate answer.

At midnight he surrendered to apparent failure and threw himself on his bed. Finally he fell into a heavy sleep.

Then the miracle happened.

''In the early hours of the morning before dawn there emerged, in one illuminous moment, a visual picturization of

Jesus, so clear and definite. And it appeared to me that I was seated at the drawing board with the completed drawing before me," says Sallman.

So real was the picturization that Sallman was soon wide awake.

Hastily he went upstairs to his studio and made a thumbnail sketch before the image disappeared from his mind's eye. The next day he made an enlarged charcoal drawing which he completed in time to make the deadline.

The Sunday school paper cover captured some attention but was soon forgotten. But the idea of picturizing a manly Christ persisted with Sallman. Largely for his own amusement he decided to make an oil painting of the sketch. When it was completed, he placed it over the piano at his home.

One day, two representatives of a church publishing house came to interview him on the possibility of doing some work for the publishing house. When Sallman let them in the door both stopped abruptly to look at the picture of the head of Christ.

"This is exactly what we have been searching for," they said. With Sallman's permission, Fred M. Bates and Anthony W. Kriebel began the publication and distribution of the "Head of Christ."

By now the U.S. was deeply involved in World War II. Quickly the Head of Christ became a symbol of hope for the men of the armed forces. More than 6 million copies were sent to men in Army, Navy and Air Force units all over the world.

Even in far-flung battle areas miracles accompanied the painting. Two Americans captured in a skirmish were being hurried back to Japanese lines for interrogation. Bayonets prodded the GIs in the back and they dared not turn their heads.

In an effort to buoy up his faith, one American started to softly whistle a gospel song tune. Suddenly he heard someone to the rear whistling the same tune.

Turning his head slightly, he heard a voice whispering in broken English.

"You Christian? We Christian too. We know song you whistle. You turn quick, grab our guns. We surrender. No want to fight you."

The scheme worked. The Americans were able to take their willing captors back through their own lines and into the hands of the American forces. Here they made an amazing discovery: The Japanese belonged to a Christian mission in Tokyo, the American to a church in Boston which had sent a large picture of Sallman's Head of Christ to the mission. The two shook hands as if feeling a covenant of brotherhood in Christ and a lasting friendship was formed.

A stream of never-ending miracles appears to follow Sallman's Head of Christ.

Reprinted by permission from Christian Life Magazine. Article by William McDermott copyright March 1963. Christian Life Inc., Gunderson Drive and Schmale Road, Wheaton, Il. 60187.

But when they deliver you up, take no thought how or what ye shall speak: for it shall be given you in that same hour what ye shall speak. For it is not ye that speak, but the spirit of your Father which speaketh to you.

Matthew 10:19-20

But I say unto you, love your enemies, bless them that curse you, do good to them that hate you, and pray for them which despitefully use you, and persecute you. *Matthew 5:44*

* * * * *

What to Do About Mistakes

Catherine Marshall is the author of many great books: A Man Called Peter; To Live Again; Beyond Ourselves; *and* Christy. *She is also the editor of several books of prayers and sermons of her late husband, Peter Marshall. She is nationally known, not only for her writings, but through the very successful movie of* A Man Called Peter *and from her TV appearances and lectures.*

It was during a period when an awareness of my own mistakes and wrong turnings gave me a sense of isolation from God. As I sat in a living room chair pondering this, there came to me a deep interior experience. I did not fall asleep, so this was no dream. Nor was it an otherworldly "vision." It seemed real, as real as the fabric on the chair, or the Florida sunlight pouring through the windows, or the trilling of a mockingbird in a tree outside. Suddenly, I felt the presence of Jesus.

"We're going on a journey," He told me.

Soon we were in a long, long room, like a throne room. Crowds of people lined the walls on either side. As we walked the length of the room approaching One whom I knew to be God, the Father, I spotted in the crowd those I love who have gone on before me: my father, Peter Marshal, my grandson Peter Christopher—now not a baby, but a small boy, blond and dear.

Then I looked down at myself: to my horror I was dressed in rags—torn, unwashed filthy. When we stopped before the throne, I could not even look up. I had never felt so unworthy.

In the same instant Jesus spread wide the voluminous robe He was wearing, completely covering me with it. (Interestingly, this was no kingly robe, rather, the roughest homespun material. I understood that until all His children are brought to glory, He continues to wear the robe of His humanity.)

"Now," He told me, "my Father does not see you at all—only Me. Not your sins, but My righteousness. I cover for you."

But we are all as an unclean thing, and all our righteousnesses are as filthy rags: and we all do fade as a leaf: and our iniquities, like the wind, have taken us away.

Isaiah 64:6

I will greatly rejoice in the Lord, my soul shall be joyful in my God; for he hath clothed me with the garments of salvation, he hath covered me with the robe of righteousness, as a bridegroom decketh himself with ornaments, and as a bride adorneth herself with her jewels.

Isaiah 61:10

* * * * *

How Pentecost Came
to Los Angeles

Frank Bartelman was converted in 1893 and left the farm to work for the Lord. After having spent two years in mission work in the north, he arrived in Los Angeles in 1904 penniless, and lived by faith. Bartelman was privileged to see and experience the early blessing of the "latter rain" outpouring at the old "Power House," Azusa Street Mission. In Los Angeles he started street meetings, pastored churches and traveled as an evangelist. He gives the following account:

One evening, July 3, I felt strongly impressed to go to the little Peniel Hall in Pasadena to pray. There I found Brother Boehmer ahead of me. He had also been led of God to the hall. We prayed for a spirit of revival for Pasadena until the burden became well nigh unbearable. I cried out like a woman in birthpangs. The spirit was interceding through us. Finally the burden left us. After a little time of quiet waiting,

77

a great calm settled down upon us. Then suddenly, without premonition, the Lord Jesus himself revealed himself to us. He seemed to stand directly between us, so close we could have reached out our hand and touched him. But we did not dare to move. I could not even look. In fact, I seemed all spirit. His presence seemed more real, if possible, than if I could have seen and touched Him naturally. I forgot I had eyes or ears. My spirit recognized Him. A heaven of divine love filled and thrilled my soul. Burning fire went through me. In fact my whole being seemed to flow down before Him, like wax before the fire. I lost all consciousness of time or space, being conscious only of His wonderful presence. I worshipped at His feet. It seemed a veritable "mount of transfiguration." I was lost in the pure Spirit.

For some time He remained with us. Then slowly He withdrew His presence. We would have been there yet had He not withdrawn. I could not doubt His reality after that experience. Brother Boehmer experienced largely the same thing. We were almost afraid to speak or breathe when we came back to our surroundings. The Lord had said nothing to us, but only ravished our spirits by His presence. He had come to strengthen and assure us for His service. We knew now we were workers with Him, fellowshippers of His sufferings, in the ministry of "soul travail." Real soul travail is just as definite in the spirit, as natural human birth pangs. The simile is almost perfect in its sameness. No soul is ever born without this. All true revivals of salvation come this way.

The sun was up next morning before we left the hall. But the night had seemed but half an hour. The presence of God eliminates all sense of time. With Him all is eternity. It is "eternal life." God knows no time. This element is lost in heaven. This is the secret of time appearing to pass so swiftly in all nights of real prayer. Time is superseded. The element of eternity is there. For days that marvelous presence seemed to walk by my side. The Lord Jesus was so real. I could scarcely take up with human conversation again. It seemed so crude and empty. Human spirits seemed so harsh, earthly fellowship a torment. How far we are naturally from the gentle spirit of Christ!

I spent the following day in prayer, going to Smale's church in the evening, where I had a ministry in intercession. Heavenly peace and joy filled my soul. Jesus was so real. Doubts and fears cannot abide in His presence.

I kept going day and night to different missions, exhorting continually to prayer, and faith for the revival. Spent another whole night with Brother Boehmer in prayer. One night at the New Testament Church, during a deep spirit of prayer on the congregation, the Lord came suddenly so near that we could feel His presence as though He were closing in on us around the edges of the meeting. Two-thirds of the people sprang to their feet in alarm, and some ran hurriedly out of the house, even leaving their hats behind them, almost scared out of their senses. There was no demonstration in the natural out of the ordinary to cause this fright. It was a supernatural manifestation of His nearness. What would such do if they saw the Lord?

From *How Pentecost Came to Los Angeles* By Frank Bartelman. Used with permission.

Spare thy people, O LORD . . .

Joel 2:17

*   *   *   *   *

The Gentle Breeze of Jesus
Mel Tari was first heard in the United States in 1970 after five years of ministry in Indonesia. His first book, Like a Mighty Wind, *has sold more than half a million copies in eleven languages. He and his American wife, Nona, make their home in Soe, Timor.*

We had been working hard on the island of Semau for several months. But it was a real battle, because, you see, Semau is famous for being the stronghold of the witch doctors. The demonic power there is just indescribable. If the witch doctors don't like someone, they will pray to the demons and ask them to make their enemy very sick. Or sometimes if they're mad enough, the pagan priests, as we call them, will ask the demons to send lightning out of heaven and strike the enemy dead. The worst part about it is that the demonic power really works; the pagan priests get what they ask for.

But praise God, the Lord has all power over Satan, and He was really blessing our ministry. At least two hundred people had gotten saved. And at least ten of these wicked witch doctors had really repented and come to Jesus. We had some big, blazing bonfires when they burned all their djimata ("fetishes") and the other demonic stuff they use in their worship.

The Lord Jesus was also busy healing people I remember there was a little kid who was born blind, and some men with huge, swollen stomachs—they looked like they were either pregnant or else had swallowed big balloons. And besides these there was a bunch of other sick people the Lord Jesus healed too.

But to be honest, I have to admit that we were really dead tired. The two other guys on my team were sort of sick because we had been working so hard day and night.

But can you imagine what my precious Jesus did? He's such a wonderful Master. He doesn't ever treat us like an old workhorse, but I believe He wants us to have fun serving Him. Well, one night after the meeting was finally over, after we had prayed for the last sick person to be healed, and after the last little old lady had finally gone home to bed, Jesus told us to go outside the church and sit down on the grass.

That night the moon was glowing high in the sky. It seemed to me that she was a royal queen on her throne, and the shimmering clouds all around were her long, flowing robes. She was splashing silver down on all the coconut palm trees that were gazing up at her. While I watched, she drenched the dainty bamboos with her crystal light until they were glowing like a string of pearls. The whole world had become a tropical fairyland; I couldn't help being captured by its beauty.

"My faithful sons," the Lord said to us, "I'm going to give you a little treat. I want to reward you for being such good helpers. Now look at the moon. I'm going to show you a special little 'film,' and the moon will be the screen." (Jesus was going to give each of us a vision. But the wonderful thing was that He gave all three of us the same vision at the same time.)

At first we didn't see anything. But as soon as we prayed, the Lord must have given us heavenly eyes or something, and wow! I'll tell you, I had never before seen such a sight.

There on the "screen" Jesus had painted some pretty green hills with a little blue stream bubbling between them. And there were lots of nice tall trees standing around raising their big leafy arms up to heaven. Then we noticed that Jesus was sitting on a big rock dressed in shepherd's clothes. All around his feet were a whole lot of cute little lambs. They were eating and sleeping, and some were hopping around playing with each other. All of a sudden Jesus stood up and started walking. All the lambs followed Him. Pretty soon they all disappeared over the other side of the hill.

Then the Lord showed us "scene two." Oh, it was just too precious for words. We saw a little lost lamb all alone, lying on the grass crying. Then the Shepherd came and picked it up in His big strong arms and held it against His heart. The little guy looked nervous at first, but the Shepherd patted him and whispered in his ears and smoothed his curly wool. Pretty soon the lamb wiggled around a little bit, and then he cuddled down in the Shepherd's arms and went to sleep.

Oh, if only you could have seen Jesus' face as He looked

81

down at His little lamb. It was so tender and full of compassion and He was smiling the sweetest smile. He looked so happy—as if He had found His most valuable treasure.

The longer I looked at Jesus the more beautiful He became to me. But it was His eyes that really captured me. They were just so full of love—it seemed like I could almost see love pouring out of them like a fountain. When I really gazed deep into them, I almost felt like I was looking through the windows of His heart. What I saw there was so wonderful, so amazing, that it took my breath away.

His heart was like an infinitely big garden full of sweetness and a laughing, sunshiny kind of joy. There were lots of pretty flowers and trees all over Jesus' heart-garden. They were being bathed in a fountain of pure, golden love. They were just sparkling with joy, as if they were thrilled to be alive, thrilled to belong to Jesus. I know that what I saw there in Jesus' heart was so wonderful that I longed to live there forever and ever.

I tell you, the thrill of Jesus' love was indescribably precious to me—much more precious than all those other miracles I had seen Him do. In fact I had almost forgotten about them because my Lord Himself was so much more wonderful. I know you would have felt the same way.

From *Gentle Breeze of Jesus* by Mel and Nona Tari. Reprinted with permission of Creation House Publishers, copyright © 1974.

And to know the love of Christ, which passeth knowledge, that ye might be filled with all the fulness of God.

Ephesians 3:19

He shall feed his flock like a shepherd: he shall gather the lambs with his arm, and carry them in his bosom, and shall gently lead those that are with young.

Isaiah 40:11

I will feed them in a good pasture, and upon the high mountains of Israel shall their fold be: there shall they lie in a good fold, and in a fat pasture shall they feed upon the mountains of Israel. I will feed my flock, and I will cause them to lie down, saith the Lord God. I will seek that which was lost, and bring again that which was driven away, and will bind up that which was broken, and will strengthen that which was sick: but I will destroy the fat and the strong; I will feed them with judgment.

Ezekiel 34:14-16

*　*　*　*　*

Fire, Rose, and a Feast
Fred Steinmann is a preacher and famous evangelist from Lockport, Illinois.

When I was a boy I lived with my parents on a farm near Joliet, Illinois. I spent much time working with my dad on the farm. One day he told me he was going to the cornfield to husk corn and that he wanted me to stay and work at the barn.

Several hours later my dad came running from the cornfield weeping. He said, "Come to the house with me, son, I want to tell you something that happened in the cornfield."

He told me the following: "While I was in the cornfield a great bright light came down around me and I became so fearful that I fell down on my face and tried to cover my eyes from this light, but it was impossible. The light was as bright and penetrating under the clods of soil as it was above it. I looked up to call on God and there stood Jesus. I said to Him, 'I cannot look upon your face because I am a sinful man.' I repent of all my sins right there and then Jesus touched me. I said to Him, I cannot speak good English but I have a boy I will give to you and he can preach for you.' I felt that this was pleasing to the Lord."

God showed my father right then that someday I would be preaching the gospel.

Later in life, after my conversion, I was lonely, sad, and heavy hearted. The closer I got to God the more trouble I had. My sister took care of me those days.

One day while working in the field, I sat down to rest and read the Bible. I read, "Out of heaven I will instruct thee and cause thee to hear my voice, out of the midst of the great fire you will hear His voice." God was speaking to Moses. I believed that God was speaking to me and that He would teach me and tell me things from heaven. I sincerely believed this, but I didn't know how it would be done.

Some months later in the early spring, I was up in the hayloft praying as this was a habit of mine. This day as I was talking to Jesus I told Him that I would not come up into the hayloft any more, but that I still loved Him and would read my Bible. Then I began to pitch hay and as I pushed my fork into the stack of hay, I looked up and saw a large beautiful rose appear above the hay. The petals began to open up and as they opened tongues of fire shot from them to the top of the barn. I was afraid the barn would catch on fire as it was full of hay and alfalfa.

What a horrible sight watching the tongues of fire and flames shooting into the air. Then out of the rose and flames came a figure of a man. I realized it was Jesus. As He looked at me, He moved slowly toward me and said, "Go preach the gospel and I will be with you." His eyes caught my eyes and I said, "Yes, Lord, I will go." After that the vision lifted and Jesus disappeared.

A few years later, during the Depression, I was preaching in the slums of 30th and State Street of Chicago, Illinois. Many days I would be without food and sometimes had to sleep in hallways. One day I was in the Chicago Loop, hungry and with only five cents in my pocket. I saw a little restaurant that posted a menu which included a five-cent bowl of soup.

I went in and a waitress came, looking at me as though I were some sort of strange creature. She asked what I would have and I told her just a bowl of soup. She asked what I wanted for the rest of my meal. I repeated, "Just the soup."

In a few minutes she brought the soup and platters of food. Without a word she placed a feast before me and I said only a word of thanks to the Lord. As I started to eat, Jesus appeared across the table from me, just as plain as He had in the rose in the barnyard. He raised His hands as in blessing, then vanished.

After I had finished eating, I called the waitress and told her I had no money to pay for all the food.

"Who asked you for any money?" she snapped.

"Why did you bring all that food—and why did you look at me so strangely when I came in?" I asked.

"Well, that's a funny thing," she said, "As you walked into this place, someone said to me, 'Feed that man. Give him all he can eat, whether he can pay for it or not.' And I did."

"Do you know who it was that spoke to you?" I asked.

"No," she said, somewhat sharply.

"It was Jesus," I told her. "I saw Him while I ate. If you don't know Him, you should. Because He died for you. I don't know a thing about you, Miss, but I know you're a sinner. Whatever sins you have, Jesus died to forgive."

Tears began to come down her face and I asked her not to cry because of the people in the restaurant. Before I left, I asked her to accept the Lord into her life, and if she did, I would surely see her in heaven. As I left, she was still standing there, wiping her eyes with her apron.

As told to the compilers by Reverend Fred Steinmann. Used with permission.

But my God shall supply all your need according to his riches in glory by Christ Jesus. Now unto God and our Father be glory for ever and ever. Amen.

Philippians 4:19,20

For though I preach the gospel, I have nothing to glory of: for necessity is laid upon me; yea, woe is unto me, if I preach not the gospel!

1 Corinthians 9:16

But as we were allowed of God to be put in trust with the gospel, even so we speak; not as pleasing men, but God, which trieth our hearts.

1 Thessalonians 2:4

* * * * *

Henry Krause, ''God's Plowman''

Henry Krause, who went to be with the Lord in 1972, was president of the Krause Plow Corporation in Hutchinson, Kansas.

He built a successful business of manufacturing plows and gave more than a million dollars to God's work during his lifetime. He had many revelations and visions of Jesus.

One morning as he was seated on the side of his bed he saw the Lord Jesus.

''He was dressed in a white robe with a red scarf over His shoulder. He had His left hand on His breast and His right hand extended to me. He stood and looked at me with eyes that seemed to burn clear through me.

''He never spoke a word. He didn't have to, for I stood in the presence of Him who is 'the Word of God'—and knowledge began to pour into me. A new understanding and power of reasoning came into me. I was a totally different person. I understood people in a new way.''

Again and again the Lord would come to Brother Krause in a dream or vision, especially when problems arose, and God would teach him not only spiritual things but material things as well. He credited the Lord with giving him the ideas for new designs in plows and other farming implements.

From a magazine article, ''How $10 Was Multiplied into Millions'' by Cathy Garlit. Reprinted by permission from the *Pentecostal Evangel*, Springfield, Missouri, Vol. No. 3091.

Be careful for nothing; but in every thing by prayer and supplication with thanksgiving let your requests be made known unto God.

Philippians 4:6

And keep the charge of the Lord thy God, to walk in his ways, to keep his statutes, and his commandments, and his judgments, and his testimonies, as it is written in the law of Moses, that thou mayest prosper in all that thou doest, and whithersoever thou turnest thyself.

1 Kings 2:3

*   *   *   *   *

A Young Boy's Vision

Reverend Norris L. Wogen was the organizer and president of the first and second International Lutheran Conferences on the Holy Spirit held in Minneapolis, Minnesota. In addition, he was president of the Midwest Lutheran Conference on the Holy Spirit and chairman of the Rocky Mountain Lutheran Conference on the Holy Spirit, both in 1973. He has traveled and lectured extensively in this country and Europe.

When I was of confirmation age, between 12 and 14 years of age, I had my initial call to go into the ministry. This is rather common. In the old Evangelical Lutheran Church they had conducted a survey some years back and they discovered that about 60 percent of the ELC ministers had received their initial call of God for the ministry at confirmation age. One of my brothers who is also a pastor received his initial call to the ministry at about the same age.

It was at confirmation age that I had a vision of Jesus standing at the top of a huge golden stairway that reached into the heavens. He was standing there in His glory with long robes. On either side of this stairway there was an honor

87

guard of living angels flying up and down, giving the impression of a living ribbon. There was no sound, just the indescribable beauty of glory and majesty. My relationship to God during this time was so great that I used to pray that God would not let me be successful in anything else—that He would force me into the ministry if necessary. I never shared this vision with anyone until about two years ago. I was the 12th child in a family of 13 and knew from other experiences that I would be laughed at and this was too precious to me to be ridiculed by anyone. This vision has been a source of inspiration for me down through the years.

As told to the compilers in a personal letter from Reverend Wogen. Used with permission.

And he [Jacob] dreamed, and behold a ladder set up on the earth, and the top of it reached to heaven: and behold the angels of God ascending and descending on it. And, behold, the Lord stood above it, and said, I am the Lord God of Abraham thy father, and the God of Isaac.

Genesis 28:12-13

* * * * *

When I Saw the Lord
Walter V. Conklin is a registered real estate broker in Florida. He relates the following experience:

It happened several months before I was to face one of the most difficult trials of my life.

About midnight in my second floor apartment in Tucson, in April of 1962, I was alone, as my wife had gone to Miami, Florida, for several weeks, because of illness in her family.

I had been on my knees praying for some time, trying to determine the Lord's directive will for my life. I had retired from business, as I felt that the Lord was leading me into full-time service for Him. Now I was thinking of going back into business, as it seemed that I was getting no definite leading.

After praying for some time I got into bed; and was lying there comfortably on my back, with my hands behind my head. I began meditating on the story of Christ on the Emmaus road, of how the disciples longed for Him to tarry for the night. The more I thought of it the more I wanted to see the Savior just as He looked to them after the resurrection.

In a business-like manner I reasoned with the Lord. "Jesus," I said: "Your word says that You are the same yesterday, and today and forever; and Lord I believe it. Your word says that You are no respecter of persons; and Lord I believe it." I quoted: "I will manifest Myself to him. Thou has visited me in the night. Thine eyes shall see the King in His beauty." You said: "Ask what you will in My name, and I will do it." I went on in this vein for some time; then I said: "Lord I, too, am lonely for your company; and I am asking You, as they did: Tarry with me for the night!"

Instantly the weight of a person caused the foot of the bed to sag under His weight. Needless to say I was startled at such a sudden response; and after several seconds I opened my eyes. I knew that Jesus had sat on my bed, but I could not see Him at this time. I thanked Him for coming, closed my eyes and went to sleep for what must have been a very short time.

I was awakened by the most hideous screams and sounds that I have ever heard. Forms came swooping in from behind and to the right of me. They were darker than the darkness of the room, which was about as light as a room with moonlight, as the lights in the courtyard behind the apartment were comparable to moonlight. The screams which were individual at the start now became a chorus such as one could expect to hear in the regions of the damned. The screams were so fierce and horrible, I cannot describe them. The whole time I was wide awake, having raised myself to a position where I was leaning back on my elbows. I was rigid with fear. The demons assembled in the corner of the room, in front and to the right of me. This was not my first experience with demons, but the first time I had ever heard them. I wondered why they were confined to the corner of the room. For some reason I felt compelled to look to where Christ had sat on the bed. There He sat with that side of the room like daylight.

He sat a little to the left of the center of the foot of the bed. He watched the demons, with His eyes going back and forth, not turning His head, but His eyes only. His left leg was flung over His right knee. His hands were resting on His knee. He sat very erect, with His head tilted upward. The position in which He was sitting presented a perfect view of His profile. Only one who has had an open vision of our Lord can possibly realize the inadequacy of words to describe Him.

His hair is luxuriant, and raven black (Song of Solomon 5:11) falling a little below His shoulders. His hair has a soft refined look, and the abundance of it gives the impression of slight waves. Both His hair and beard have a sheen. His nose is perfectly straight. His eyes, which fascinated me so, are very alert, not large but average size, and are a very dark brown. His complexion is flawless and a light olive in color. No blood showed in His cheeks, and I remembered it was left in the Holy of Holies. He is lean and slender. He is not muscular as some have speculated because of His years in the carpenter shop. I would estimate His weight at about one hundred sixty-five to one hundred seventy pounds. I would judge His height at about five-foot-ten to five-foot-eleven. I could see Him breathe and occasionally sway slightly, as you or I might while sitting in that position on a bed. His completely white robe reached to His feet, and the sleeves, to His hands. He is a handsome Jew in His early thirties!

He was not a stranger, but as one of the family, as if I had known Him forever. It was breath-taking to see His beautiful black hair contrasted against His white robe. I had always thought His hair would be brown or chestnut, as is so often depicted by artists.

It is almost impossible to describe my feelings at this time to be frightened almost to death: and then to turn, and see the Prince of Peace sitting about three feet from me. When I had asked Him to manifest Himself to me I thought that He would probably appear across the room from me. It never occurred to me that He would sit on the bed, but how like our Savior to identify Himself with us. The Good Shepherd was faithfully guarding His sheep. I felt like a little boy again; every care, worry and anxiety had slid from me like a mantle. I had absolutely no fear of the demons. After watching Him for some time I again turned to look at the demons. They were hemmed in by His eyes. I turned to Him again; and after watching His eyes for some time, I leaned back and went to sleep.

You might think that you would have talked to Him, or reached out and touched Him, but at such a time one is too amazed, and can stare only in a dumbfounded manner it seems. Perhaps you would not have leaned back and gone to sleep with the Saviour still sitting there. This had bothered me a great deal since, but the peace and security was so great it was not possible to stay awake.

There is hardly a day that I don't recall this wonderful night. He reminds me often that He is just as near always even though I don't see Him. Also, I learned that we are to be most vigilant because of the enemy. It seems harder to wait for His coming now since I have seen Him.

From a tract written by Walter V. Conklin. Used with permission.

And his father Zacharias was filled with the Holy Ghost, and prophesied, saying, Blessed be the Lord God of Israel; for he hath visited and redeemed his people, and hath raised up an horn of salvation for us in the house of his servant David; As he spake by the mouth of his holy prophets, which have been since the world began: That we should be saved from our enemies, and from the hand of all that hate us; To perform the mercy promised to our fathers, and to remember his holy covenant; The oath which he sware to our father Abraham, That he would grant unto us, that we being delivered out of the hand of our enemies might serve him without fear, In holiness and righteousness before him, all the days of our life.

Luke 1:67-75

*   *   *   *   *

Liberian Native

Clara Lewis has served in Sinoe, Liberia, six degrees above the equator, for forty years.

Clara Lewis, a missionary in Liberia, West Africa was accustomed to having many of her converts come to her for prayer when they needed healing or for the salvation of their loved ones. James, one of the nationals, married his deceased brother's wife (according to heathen custom) but was concerned because she was not a Christian. Mary was many years older than James and often ridiculed her husband because of his faith in the Lord Jesus Christ. She was an artist at nagging and made life miserable for her husband.

One day Mary became very ill and James came to the mission and asked us to pray. The entire church prayed for Mary's salvation in the evening service. The Lord answered in a very wonderful way and Mary was saved and healed.

Mary had a wonderful vision of heaven and we were really surprised when she tried to explain what heaven was like. She had never attended the services or heard anyone preach the Gospel.

We asked her if they had lamps or lanterns in heaven. She replied, "No, they did not need lamps because the whole place was full of light. Jesus was there and His presence lit up the whole place. The Light shined past the sun, the stars and the moon.

"His clothes were white and shining. We always thought

your clothes were pretty and white but now your clothes seem almost dirty."

This heavenly vision proved a great help and blessing to Mary and she loved and served the Lord Jesus Christ and was a blessing to many. She often longed and prayed to join the heavenly host and praise the Lord as they did in heaven.

As told by Clara Lewis to the compilers in a letter. Used with permission.
And there shall be no night there; and they need no candle, neither light of the sun; for the Lord God giveth them light: and they shall reign for ever and ever.

Revelation 22:5

* * * * *

"Jesus, Where Are You?"

The Reverend Nadine Sutliff Peterson was a child evangelist in Chicago, Illinois, and is now pastoring the Philadelphia Church, Bradenton, Florida. The following account tells how Reverend Peterson met the Lord:

I was 13 years old and pretty uptight about this "salvation" bit. I wanted it, of course (at least enough to go to heaven on) but I also had a strong desire for the fun in the world. I had taken all the prescribed steps toward making a decision for Christ but still had this "unsure" uneasiness in my heart.

That night the evangelist had made a direct appeal to anyone who had not settled this question for once and for all and I had responded. Kneeling at the altar that night, I bargained with God—"Now, if there really is a personal knowledge of Jesus as Lord and Savior, I want it. If not, I'm going to forget this whole business."

It was then I saw Jesus.

Mom and Dad said I never left the altar and never made a sound. But it seemed to me that I had jumped up from the

93

altar, run out of the church, up and down the streets searching for Jesus. And it seemed to me I was screaming at the top of my lungs, "Jesus, Jesus, where are you????"

It seemed to me that I looked everywhere—gave up—and ran back into the church— knelt back down at the altar and said in despair: "Jesus, where are you? I can't find you anywhere!"

And there He was. Just like the lovely pictures I had seen of Him. In His long, white, loose robe, with his long, beautiful hair and sweet smile, with His hands held out to me lovingly.

Mom and Dad said I never made a sound. But it seemed to me I just relaxed and said, "Well, there you were all the time and I've been running all around trying to find you."

And the more I relaxed and worshiped Him, the closer He came and the smaller He became. Closer and smaller. Closer and smaller—until He was about an inch tall!! Then He reached out, opened the door of my heart and jumped in! Closed the door behind Him. Inside my heart, He hunched Himself over, spread Himself out and filled every "nook and cranny" of my heart.

Talk about glory! Talk about assurance of salvation!

This vision came to my searching heart several years ago, but I love Him more than ever today. The unshakeable faith the Lord Jesus planted in my heart through the vision He gave me that night has put me right in the middle of service to Him where I expect to remain until He calls me upward.

As told to the compilers by Reverend Nadine Peterson in a letter. Used with permission.

Behold, I stand at the door, and knock: if any man hear my voice, and open the door, I will come in to him, and will sup with him, and he with me.

Revelation 3:20

The Bread of Life—God's Word

Sue McConnaughay is a 26-year-old housewife from Oak Park, Illinois, married to Orly (Butch) McConnaughay, and the mother of three small children. Many can identify with her as she describes her life simply, "My marriage has been on the rocks, and I keep getting pregnant." But God is in the business of restoring marriages, and Butch and Sue have experienced this first-hand. It was during the time before the birth of her third child, when she was under doctor's orders to rest each afternoon, that she experienced this vision.

I have been having a problem in my life which is composed of many smaller problems and circumstances. I have had victory in some areas but still never seemed to get on top of the situation. My feeling was one of discouragement. After victory in one very serious problem, concerning submission to my husband, I found myself backsliding into the same thing again. I didn't know if this was the result of not being properly submissive to my husband, not understanding something the Lord was saying, or what! One afternoon after I had prayed about this, I was dozing when the Lord spoke so clearly it woke me up! He said, "Be hungry for my word." I literally felt as if I were floating, and then the Lord said, "I am the bread of life." I saw the Lord standing in front of me holding a loaf of bread on a bread board. He kept handing me one slice of bread at a time, but the loaf never got smaller! *He* is the answer to my problems! He will never run out of solutions. I was willing to do anything the Lord said, but I was expecting a drastic request on His part! Now, I'm spending more time in scripture, and less time worrying about what I'm to be doing. Psalm 34:4-10: "I sought the Lord, and he heard me, and delivered me from all my fears. They looked unto him, and were lightened: and their faces were not ashamed. This poor man cried, and the Lord heard him, and saved him out of all his troubles. The angel of the

Lord encampeth round about them that fear him, and delivereth them. O taste and see that the Lord is good: blessed is the man that trusteth in him. O fear the Lord, ye his saints: for there is no want to them that fear him. The young lions do lack, and suffer hunger: but they that seek the Lord shall not want any good thing.''

I charge thee therefore before God, and the Lord Jesus Christ, who shall judge the quick and the dead at his appearing and his kingdom; Preach the word; be instant in season, out of season; reprove, rebuke, exhort with all longsuffering and doctrine.

2 Timothy 4:1-2

* * * * *

Child of Jesus

This beautiful experience has stayed with Irma Foster throughout her whole life. She has been a dedicated child of God and brave through many hardships which she has encountered as an adult. Mrs. Foster now resides in the Christian Handicapped Home In Walworth, Wisconsin.

Because of necessity, my older sister and I were taken to Europe to stay with my grandparents and left there while my mother came back to America. When we returned to America three years later I was 5½. My parents seemed unfamiliar to me, almost strangers, and I was a very unhappy, confused little girl. I had trouble adjusting and as I was the youngest in the family I was often punished for, what seemed to me, even the slightest mistakes. One day, after a very trying morning, when I was 6 years old, my parents went out, taking my sister with them and leaving me home for punishment. We lived in the big city on the second floor on a street car line next to the elevated train station on Chicago Avenue. I went to the front window, put my elbows on the window sill and stared out of the window and down to the street where people were rushing back and forth going places. I was very sad and finally I put my head down on my arms on the window sill and cried until it seemed that my heart would break. I felt that no one loved me.

After I felt better I raised my head and looked up to the sky. I was very astonished to see a shining figure, just the head and shoulder, of what I later came to know as Jesus. It shown brightly and I was scared and fearful but as I looked at the eyes I became conscious of love pouring out to me, such love as I had never experienced before, and a wonderful warmth enfolded me. I was filled with the ecstasy of joy. I looked down to the street and wondered why none of them saw what I did. His eyes also looked down to them and I was conscious of a message:

"These too are my children."

From that time on, whenever things went wrong, I went to my room to be alone to think about my experience and I always felt the wonderful warmth and love enfold me, reassure me and help me to understand, forgive and try harder to be good.

As told to the author in a letter from Irma Foster. Used with permission.

At the same time came the disciples unto Jesus, saying, Who is the greatest in the kingdom of heaven? And Jesus called a little child unto him, and set him in the midst of them, And said, Verily I say unto you, Except ye be converted, and become as little children, ye shall not enter into the kingdom of heaven. Whosoever therefore shall humble himself as this little child, the same is greatest in the kingdom of heaven. And whoso shall receive one such little child in my name receiveth me.

Matthew 18:1-5

And all thy children shall be taught of the Lord; and great shall be the peace of thy children.

Isaiah 54:13

Now therefore hearken unto me, O ye children: for blessed are they that keep my ways.

Proverbs 8:32

Better is a poor and a wise child than an old and foolish king, who will no more be admonished.

Ecclesiastes 4:13

*   *   *   *   *

Witnessing

Lucile Huyssen, one of the compilers of this volume, tells of an experience which showed her the importance of witnessing for Jesus.

While attending a Full Gospel Business Men's convention breakfast at the Conrad Hilton in Chicago, I was standing with the audience singing and praising God. I had my eyes closed worshiping the Lord when much to my surprise Jesus appeared to me, but all I could see was the lower part of His face. Yet I knew it was He. His lips were closed and without a smile, giving a very somber impression.

I opened my eyes and looked around, thinking that I must be imagining this. When I closed my eyes again the vision was still there and remained for some time.

Then I asked the Lord why He was not smiling or did not speak and He plainly showed me that this was to portray to me that I had not been witnessing or speaking for Him.

I was amazed to think that Jesus would point out to me my failure to witness for Him. For years I had wanted to be an effective witness for Christ but I didn't have the courage. This vision changed my whole life. After seeing this vision I had an intense desire to witness for Christ and to serve Him.

I asked the Holy Spirit to guide me completely in witnessing. I found that it was easy to pass out tracts and leave them in conspicuous places but speaking of Christ to others was more difficult.

By taking a correspondence course in witnessing I learned to let the Holy Spirit take over and witness through me. He will always give you an opportunity to witness at the right and proper time in the perfect way. I found it was a matter of learning to depend on Him.

Whosoever therefore shall confess me before men, him will I confess also before my Father which is in heaven. But whosoever shall deny me before men, him will I also deny before my Father which is in heaven.

Matthew 10:32-33

Go ye therefore, and teach all nations, baptizing them in the name of the father, and of the Son, and of the Holy Ghost.

Matthew 28:19-20

But ye shall receive power, after that the Holy Ghost is come upon you: and ye shall be witnesses unto me both in Jerusalem, and in all Judea and in Samaria, and unto the uttermost part of the earth.

Acts 1:8

* * * * *

Acceptance

Richard H. Rice served as an assistant secretary for a consulting engineer firm in Bethesda, Maryland. He is a member of St. Paul's Methodist Church in Kensington, Maryland, and an officer in the Fort Meade Laurel chapter of the Full Gospel Business Men's Fellowship International.

The glory and grace of God began in my life when I was born July 26, 1945, with Ataxia Cerebral Palsy, and has continued through the years, during which I have been continually healed of the brain damage which I obtained at birth. This healing is now complete beyond my wildest hopes.

It was at the beginning of my junior year when the

realization came that I was in serious trouble and headed straight for disaster if something were not done, and done quickly. This "something" came during study hall one evening in the form of a poem, which made a definitive and decisive point in showing me that which I sought could be found only in Jesus Christ. That summer I worked at a Christian camp for underprivileged children from the Washington, D.C. area. On my twenty-first birthday I went out for a celebration with another counselor after everyone had gone to bed. We returned around 11:30 just as a storm was beginning to brew. At midnight, a streak of lightning brightened the entire sky, and above the cross on a nearby mountain there appeared to us a vision of Christ frowning. I interpreted this to mean that I should turn around and accept the disciplined way of the Lord or face ultimate disaster. At the same time, God assured me that if I stopped warring against Him, salvation would be mine. One week later, however, not having yet followed through as I should, I awoke in the middle of the night with an anxiety attack. This really frightened me, and prepared my heart for the Lord Jesus to come in and start the cleansing process.

This event took place November 18, 1967, following a Sunday evening service in a Baptist church in New Hampshire. The spiritual "ice" melted, my heart became soft, and I invited Jesus Christ into my life as my personal Lord and Saviour. Instantaneously I felt a great weight lifted from my shoulders and realized I was being freed from the degradation of hatred which had so long ruled my life. I felt peace and a wave of joy like an ocean flowing through my entire body. One month later Jesus revealed to me that I no longer needed cigarettes for a companion or to calm my nerves, and within three days I went from one-and-a-half packs a day to none.

Enter ye in at the strait gate: for wide is the gate, and broad is the way, that leadeth to destruction, and many there be which go in thereat: Because strait is the gate, and narrow is the way, which leadeth unto life, and few there be that find it.

Matthew 7:13-14

* * * * *

I Worked with Hell's Angels

Phil Smith was a gangster and gang leader who lived by the fist and the switchblade. By age twenty he was a confirmed alcoholic.

Through a co-worker on an assembly line, he first witnessed the power of God. Later the Lord miraculously delivered and set him free from many sins, including alcohol, nicotine, lust, hate and murder.

After his conversion, he traveled extensively to tell the Good News. In a street ministry, he rode among the Hell's Angel's in a new motorcycle gang named the "Christ's Patrol." Many have been lead to the Lord and lives changed through this ministry.

Why did I throw my life away and become a gangster? It was partly because of my home life. As far back as I can remember my father beat my mother. This caused hatred and resentment to fill my heart even before I was old enough to start school. It made me hate the world. When I was a lad of nine my mother, without any advance notice, brought in a stranger and told me that he was my "new father."

Having no home life I found the wrong kind of friends in school. Soon the boys were looking to me for instructions. Soon I had my own dance band. We were playing for the lodges and night clubs. I was involved in street gangs of Dayton.

Because of personal problems with a girl I began to drink. For three years I was drunk every night. A boy that gets drunk may do anything. To get drunk is to yield to the devil for him to use you at his will.

While still in my teens I was a progressive jazz musician. I traveled with many jazz combos for nearly two years. I joined Bobby Wertz's Orchestra and then spent my time playing in the plush night spots.

By this time the bitterness in my heart had multiplied many times. I began to form gangs in the Southern Ohio streets. Then it spread to other cities. I led the "rumbles" around Indian Lake. Every night for two long years my skin on my face began to tighten. I got so I could not smile. Soon I was completely demon possessed. In my heart was murder, lust, hate, and things I dare not put on paper. I hated and wanted to kill the people I met.

I soon began to live by the switchblade. I was only contented when I could beat people into a pulp. I used tire tools, chains, clubs, knucks, or most anything I could find. If I had no gun or brickbat I used my bare fist. I still carry scars where I smashed windows with my fist. If my enemy was in a car with the glasses rolled up that made no difference. With my fist I went through that car window. I used to become so angry at stop signs that I would smash them bare-handed. Soon everyone knew that I looked just like the devil himself. They were afraid. Even hardened exconvicts and killers ran from me when they saw me. They shunned me as people did Legion in the country of the Gadarenes (Mark 5:5).

Some say you can't become unconscious when you drink whiskey and vodka, but I did for days at a time. I went through what they called "lost weekends" when I would completely lose my mind. Many people went to the electric chair because of "lost weekends," but somehow God spared me for a reason. By His grace I am what I am. I would return many times with my face and fists burst. I looked at the dried blood and wondered where it came from. I did not know who was killed or hurt on that trip.

Running 120 miles per hour in a friend's car I remembered

rolling over many times, wishing every time that the car turned that I would die. One of my best friends was killed because of Russian Roulette, but I was spared. Many times my life was hanging on a thread so to speak, when we played "chicken." Two cars would meet each other running head on. The boy or girl that left the car first was called "chicken." Many were killed. God let me live to tell of hell on earth.

I was a confirmed alcoholic in my twenties. When I spit on the sidewalk the spit was nearly all alcohol. Then I reasoned that if I stayed too busy to drink I would get better. To prepare physically for my enemies from other gangs I began lifting 120 pound weights. I could let any man hit my stomach. He could not hurt me, my muscles were so strong and tight.

I had to work hard and long and go through a lot of danger in order to keep up my reputation and remain a leader. To keep up my muscles I worked on an assembly line where I lifted heavy parts. As I was working there a man mentioned Jesus to me day after day. God had him spotted at the right place.

The devil in me became angry one day. I said, "If you mention the name of Jesus one more time I'll hit you so hard that you will never stop rolling." I threatened and cursed him. I thought that my new "friend" would be afraid of me and stop that "foolishness." He mentioned that name to me once more in a few days. I was ready for him. As I started to hit him he threw me over his head and let me land anyway I happened to fall. He happened to be a former Judo instructor from Germany.

When he found what he had done he picked me up and said, "Pal, I am sorry. I should not have done that. I am a Christian. I should trust the Lord. Go ahead and do anything you want to do to me. I won't do anything." He stood there with his hands beside him looking into my face.

There I stood looking into the face of a man I had never met before. I could not help but admire a man like that who would stand up for what he thought was right. At the same time I knew I could not "chicken out" there. My gang members were working on that job. There they were looking on the drama. I knew if I did not whip that man my "buddies" would whip me. They would beat me up and leave me for dead. They would never trust me again.

Just here I saw my first miracle in my life. As I started to swing God bound my fist. I could not make the punch, for I was chained! I could not see. God had blinded me! When my eyesight and reason returned I found myself shaking hands with the first real "Christian" I had seen. The gang members did not kill me. Evidently God must have bound their hands, too.

I never got over this miracle. I began to do research. I began to investigate. My new friend told me, as he helped me wash up, about a deliverance revival, where miracles took place. He said that the blind saw, the deaf heard, and the lame walked.

One night I slipped in on such a meeting. As I was watching, waiting and wondering, I saw a blanket coming down from heaven. A corner of it touched me. Slowly it all covered me. I was cleansed. I suddenly was set free from sin, including alcohol, nicotine, lust, hate, and murder. Old things had passed away. All things had become new. That was the greatest miracle of the revival.

I said, "God, let me know that you are real." God spoke to me seven times in one second. "Go into the ministry." Just then the evangelist said, "God has just spoken to a young man in the back and given him a call."

Later I saw a vision of Christ for thirty minutes. The Lord sent me to five different foreign countries to tell the glad news. In every place God worked wonders. I was six months in each country. I went from coast to coast all over America telling this glad news.

About the time I thought I was "established" in the ministry, God spoke again, "I am sending you back out into the streets." Now my ministry is to the other ninety percent of the people that never attend church. At this time we are planning five centers in five major cities, including the Bronx, Cleveland and Chicago. We will be working with the "Hell's Angels" on the West Coast.

From the *Voice of Deliverance*, Dallas, Texas, "I Work with the Hell's Angels," September, 1968. Used with permission.

And one of the malefactors which were hanged railed on him, saying, If thou be Christ, save thyself and us. But the other answering rebuked him, saying, Dost not thou fear God, seeing thou art in the same condemnation? And we indeed justly; for we receive the due reward of our deeds: but this man hath done nothing amiss. And he said unto Jesus, Lord, remember me when thou comest into thy kingdom. And Jesus said unto him, Verily I say unto thee, Today shalt thou be with me in paradise.

Luke 23:39-43

Come now, and let us reason together, saith the LORD: though your sins be as scarlet, they shall be as white as snow; though they be red like crimson they shall be as wool.

Isaiah 1:18

As far as the east is from the west, so far hath he removed our transgressions from us.

Psalm 103:12

* * * * *

Visions of Jesus

Joe Pawlak is a layman, employed as an engineer in a south side factory in Chicago, Illinois.

I had a meeting with Jesus Christ in May, 1969. It was a beautiful warm, sunny day. I realize now that it was God who led me to go down to the lake front to eat my lunch that day. Many were sitting on the benches eating their noonday lunch.

The fishermen were coming in with their catch, displaying the huge fish they had caught. I took my lunch out and was about to pour my coffee and have a bit to eat when I looked out across Lake Michigan and saw that all things began to disappear except for a direct line onto the lake and there was Jesus walking on the water toward me. He actually seemed taller than a telephone pole.

In the vision was a dimension of beautiful color that one is not able to see with the normal eye. He was wearing sandals, a beautiful red robe and a blue cape. His hair was dark auburn to His shoulders and his eyes were of the most beautiful color that I have ever seen. It was a blue that is indescribable. He had no mustache or beard, just a tiny line of hair along the jaw line and it looked as though an artist had taken a paint brush and drawn this line from one side to the other. There was a golden aura around Jesus and as He came closer I looked into His eyes and saw love, compassion and beauty there. Oh, such loveliness!

He walked through the pier, the cars and people and stood at the hood of my car, holding his arms up as if He were praying over me and then He made the sign of the cross. The He looked to the left and disappeared.

Right then the old sinner died in me and I was born again. I did not understand all of this at the time because I had been raised a Roman Catholic and had not read the Bible. I didn't know that Jesus was appearing to people and that they were seeing visions. I didn't know that people could receive the gifts of the Spirit and speak in tongues. I didn't know that people could be healed by Jesus.

For three days and nights I wept for joy. We were advised to go to a Full Gospel Church and here they told me that speaking in tongues and having visions of Jesus was scriptural. These people encouraged me to read my Bible.

Sometimes I have seen Jesus as many as three times in one day and then three weeks may pass before I see Him again. One evening while praying in my prayer room I had a vision of the Last Supper. The apostles were sitting completely around the table and Jesus was facing me. The apostles were leaning over toward each other in conversation, but I could not hear their conversation. Jesus reached over and took a piece of bread and laid it down on His tray. Then He bowed His head, held His hands over the bread and prayed. After He made the sign of the cross He broke a piece off and put it on His plate and then passed the bread to the right. Then I noticed a pitcher passed over to Him and it seemed to be filled with a clear liquid. (The beauty of the color of this vision is beyond my ability to describe.) Then Jesus put His hands over the pitcher, prayed and made the sign of the cross. He poured some of the liquid into His cup and passed the pitcher over to the apostle at His right. My complete attention seemed to be focused on a broken part of the spout of the pitcher.

Some weeks after I had had this vision, I was speaking in a Baptist church and I mentioned how my attention had been drawn to the broken part of the spout of the pitcher. At the close of the service a man in the congregation came up to me and asked me if I had ever read the Dead Sea Scrolls. Now, remember, this was at the beginning of my ministry and I had just started reading the Bible. I had never heard of the Dead Sea Scrolls nor had I heard of the book. I told the man that I did not know what he meant and he explained that he was a theology student and had been studying the Dead Sea Scrolls and that the pitcher with the broken piece in it is mentioned in the book.

One morning during Easter week I went to my office early and found that I was the only one there. I sat at my desk looking over my work for the day and as I was shuffling through the papers everything disappeared and I found myself in a strange land. I was standing at the foot of a hill dressed in my twentieth century clothes while everyone around me, and up and down the hill was clothed in strange costumes. Then I realized that his was 2,000 years ago during the Roman Empire days.

I saw two Roman soldiers tugging on huge, heavy ropes and I wondered what they could be doing. They were straining their muscles as they pulled on these ropes. Then I noticed a third soldier standing behind a huge board. I didn't understand at this time what I was seeing but as the third soldier started pushing on this heavy board the picture began to unveil itself.

I then realized that it was the crucifixion that I was seeing. There was Jesus on the cross and these two soldiers had ropes tied to the cross and were pulling it up as the third soldier was pushing on the cross to get it into an upright position. As strange as it may seem to you, I was so engrossed in what I was viewing that my one concern was to see how they would succeed in getting the cross into an upright position. The three soldiers pushed and pulled on the cross until they got it to a hole which they had dug and then they dropped the cross down into this hole and let go of the ropes.

Can you picture our Lord hanging on the cross with all of His weight? As the cross dropped down into the hole it tore his hands and feet where they were nailed. Then I could see Jesus' face. The crown of thorns had not been placed on His head, but had been pushed into the flesh so that the blood was trickling down over His eyes and face. Oh, what a horrible, horrible sight. Jesus died for sinners.

Dear God, I am so thankful that I didn't see in the vision how they nailed Him to the cross, because I think my heart would have broken. I saw only the blood dripping from His hands and feet where He was nailed. Jesus was brutally beaten. As I looked at Him I could plainly see that there wasn't a spot on His body that wasn't bruised, black, purple, yellow and red.

As I was watching the blood run down His face, the vision moved over to the right. There I saw the three Marys kneeling down so low that their faces were buried in the ground. They were sobbing as though their hearts would break. At the time

I did not know who they were until later when I read the Bible. Then the vision moved over to the front of the cross where the people were mulling around. At the foot of the cross stood two of the soldiers, one in front and one in back, holding long lances in their hands. Then I became conscious of other people who seemed to be in shock as they lay there on their backs staring up at the sky. Others, men, women and children were sitting with their backs against the trees. . . .

Each time I share this vision with anyone, I can't help but break down and cry because it is so vivid and real to me. To think that God, our Father, would send His only begotten son to suffer and die for our sins is overwhelming. I'm so grateful to the Lord that he revealed this to me so that I can share it with you.

As personally told to the compilers by Joe Pawlak.

For I have received of the Lord that which also I delivered unto you, That the Lord Jesus, the same night in which he was betrayed, took bread: And when he had given thanks, he brake it, and said, Take, eat; this is my body, which is broken for you: this do in remembrance of me. After the same manner also he took the cup, when he had supped, saying, This cup is the new testament in my blood: this do ye, as oft as ye drink it, in remembrance of me. For as often as ye eat this bread, and drink this cup, ye do show the Lord's death till he come.

1 Corinthians 11:23-26

Let this mind be in you, which was also in Christ Jesus: Who, being in the form of God, thought it not robbery to be equal with God: But made himself of no reputation, and took upon him the form of a servant, and was made in the likeness of men: And being found in fashion as a man, humbled himself, and became obedient unto death, even the death of the cross.

Philippians 2:5-8

For I determined not to know anything among you, save Jesus Christ, and him crucified.   *1 Corinthians 2:2*

109

And you, that were sometime alienated and enemies in your mind by wicked works, yet now hath he reconciled In the body of his flesh through death, to present you holy and unblamable and unreprovable in his sight. . . .

Colossians 1:21-22

*   *   *   *   *

Compassion and Judgment

J. Hinton Massey was born in Morris, Illinois and received his early education in the Morris Public Schools.

Subsequent to his graduation from the Morris High School, he was graduated from Northwestern University School of Commerce.

He then entered Chicago Kent College of Law. Subsequent to his graduation from Chicago Kent College of Law he passed the Illinois bar examination and began practicing law in Joliet, Illinois.

Five years later he was 'born again' and about six years thereafter began his studies in religion, supporting himself by practicing law.

He holds the degrees of J.D. and L.L.D. He was ordained in 1945 and was consecrated Bishop in the Old Catholic Church in 1963. He is now pastor of St. Paul's Church in Plainfield, Illinois and at times assists clients in exparte and religious matters.

Bishop Julius H. Massey, Pastor of St. Paul's Old Catholic Church in Plainfield, Illinois, saw Jesus face to face. Several times Bishop Massey asked the Lord to give him a vision of Christ. One night while asleep he was awakened by someone gently tapping on the side of his mattress. He awakened instantly, and saw Jesus just turning to walk along the side of his bed, to go to the foot of the bed. Jesus was clothed with a dazzling white garment; His hair was auburn and came down at the back of His head to His shoulder. The bishop said His

110

face was the most beautiful face that he had ever seen, and on that face were two diametrically opposite looks. The one, the kind compassionate look of the Saviour, and the other the stern majestic look of a king.

Bishop Massey said he was speechless and after ten seconds Jesus extinguished Himself, i.e. went out like a light. The bishop then said to himself that Jesus is the Saviour of some and the judge of others, and that he could more fully understand the scripture which says that the wicked will pray for the rocks to fall on them to hide them from the face of Him who sits on the throne.

As told in a letter from Bishop Massey to the compilers Used with permission.

And the kings of the earth, and the great men, and the rich men, and the chief captains, and the mighty men, and every bondman, and every free man, hid themselves in the dens and in the rocks of the mountains; And said to the mountains and rocks, Fall on us, and hide us from the face of him that sitteth on the throne, and from the wrath of the Lamb: For the great day of his wrath is come; and who shall be able to stand?

Revelation 6:15-17

* * * * *

Afterword

If these testimonies have pointed out to you the reality of the living and loving Lord and Saviour Jesus Christ, and you wish to receive Him as your personal Lord and Saviour, you should follow the five steps below to become a Christian:

FIRST: Acknowledge you are condemned because of sin!
1. You are by nature a sinner:
   "There is none righteous, no, not one" (Romans 3:10). "For all have sinned, and come short of the glory of God" (Romans 3:23).
2. Sin has separated you from God:
   "But your iniquities have separated between you and your God, and your sins have hid his face from you, that he will not hear" (Isaiah 59:2).
3. Penalty of sin is eternal punishment:
   "In flaming fire taking vengeance on them that know not God, and that obey not the gospel of our Lord Jesus Christ: who shall be punished with everlasting destruction from the presence of the Lord, and from the glory of his power" (2 Thessalonians 1:8,9).

SECOND: Realize you must be saved from sin!
1. You must be born again:
   "Jesus answered and said unto him, Verily, verily, I say unto thee, Except a man be born again he cannot see the kingdom of God" (John 3:3).
2. You must become God's child:
   "But as many as received him to them gave he the right to become the children of God, even to them that believe on his name" (John 1:12, ASV).
3. You must become a new person:
   "Therefore if any man be in Christ, he is a new creature: old things are passed away; behold, all things are become new" (2 Corinthians 5:17).

112

THIRD: Admit you cannot save yourself from sin!
1. Your righteousness will not save you:
   "Not by works of righteousness which we have done, but according to his mercy he saved us" (Titus 3:5).
2. Your religious deeds will not save you:
   "For by grace are ye saved through faith: and that not of yourselves: it is the gift of God: not of works, lest any man should boast" (Ephesians 2:8,9).
3. Jesus alone can save you:
   "Neither is there salvation in any other; for there is none other name under heaven given among men, whereby we must be saved" (Acts 4:12).

FOURTH: Believe Jesus died for your sin!
1. Jesus' death paid the penalty for sin:
   "Who his own self bare our sins in his own body on the tree, that we, being dead to sins, should live unto righteousness: by whose stripes ye were healed" (1 Peter 2:24).
2. Jesus' blood cleanses from all sin:
   "In whom we have redemption through his blood, the forgiveness of sins, according to the riches of his grace" (Ephesians 1:7).
3. Jesus' resurrection provides eternal life:
   "But now is Christ risen from the dead, and become the first fruits of them that slept" (1 Corinthians 15:20).

FIFTH: Receive Jesus as your Savior from sin!
1. By believing on the Lord Jesus Christ:
   "Believe on the Lord Jesus Christ, and thou shalt be saved" (Acts 16:31).
2. By asking God to forgive you:
   "Come now, and let us reason together, saith the Lord: though your sins be as scarlet, they shall be as white as snow; though they be red like crimson, they shall be as wool" (Isaiah 1:18).

"Repent ye therefore, and be converted, that your sins may be blotted out" (Acts 3:19).
3. By asking God to save you:
"For whosoever shall call upon the name of the Lord shall be saved" (Romans 10:13).

Prayer of Salvation

Almighty and most merciful God, I thank You for sending Your Son, Jesus Christ, who died for my sins and arose again from the dead that I might live eternally with Him. I am truly sorry for everything that I have done wrong and I ask You to forgive me. I now ask You to make me a Christian. I open my heart to You and ask You to come in and live forever within me. I want to live for You and ask You to guide me in all my ways from this day forward. As I read Your Word, may Your Holy Spirit teach me and draw me ever closer in love to You and to my fellow man to the glory of Your Holy name. Amen.